# ...With Reading and Writing for All!

*A Common Sense Approach to Reading and Writing For Teachers and Parents*

## Louise McGrew

iUniverse, Inc.
New York   Bloomington

…With Reading and Writing for All!
A Common Sense Approach to Reading and
Writing For Teachers and Parents

*iUniverse books may be ordered through booksellers or by contacting:*

*iUniverse*
*1663 Liberty Drive*
*Bloomington, IN 47403*
*www.iuniverse.com*
*1-800-Authors (1-800-288-4677)*

*Because of the dynamic nature of the Internet, any Web addresses or links contained in
this book may have changed since publication and may no longer be valid. The views
expressed in this work are solely those of the author and do not necessarily reflect the
views of the publisher, and the publisher hereby disclaims any responsibility for them.*

*ISBN: 978-1-4502-5735-0 (sc)*
*ISBN: 978-1-4502-5736-7 (ebook)*

*Library of Congress Control Number: 2010913323*

*Printed in the United States of America*

*iUniverse rev. date: 9/23/2010*

# Dedication

This book is dedicated to some important people in my life. First, my husband Duncan McGrew, whose support and encouragement is endless. And second, to Tamara Ketscher, who not only took the time to read the original very rough draft but also gave me invaluable insight into making the book more teacher-friendly. And third, to a wonderful niece, Miranda Sorensen, who worked hard to make this book professional in its appearance.

It is also dedicated to all the students who helped me as I learned and redefined the process, as well as to those who would benefit from this approach to the reading and writing processes.

# Table of Contents

# About the Author

I have been teaching reading in one way or another for the past thirty years. I have a lifetime California teaching credential, a current reading specialist credential, a cross-cultural language academic development credential, two years of Multi-District Teachers Training designed to educate teachers in the best methods for teaching English Language Learners, a master's in education with a focus on language development and reading, a special education credential, a Clear Resource Specialist Certificate, and finally an administrative certificate. My experience consists of being a teacher for seventeen years in self-contained classes at all grade levels from kindergarten to eighth; a reading specialist for eight years; a resource specialist for six years; and a program specialist for seven years. Throughout all of my years in education, my focus has always been reading.

Because this book has been on the back burner for some time, it would be very difficult to track down my previous students and their families. So I will just share a few of the wonderful memories I have about this approach because it works and children learned to read.

One that still brings tears to my eyes occurred when I was a first-year resource specialist at a new school with all new students. An eighth-grade boy there was reading and spelling at a beginning first-grade level. This young man would not make eye contact with anyone, and he never smiled; he just walked around with his head hanging down. I had thirteen other seventh and eighth graders at about the same level. I proceeded to instruct them in the manner described in Chapters 4 and 5 At first, this boy sat in the back of the class just barely looking up for instruction. After about six weeks, he began making tentative eye contact, and after about another month, he actually elbowed another student so he could sit up front, where he sat from then on. This young man developed one of the most engaging smiles and became a participating member of his eighth-grade class. With some extra tutoring and the use of mnemonics, he passed the Constitution Test. His mother came in toward the end of school to thank me and then told me that all her son ever wanted to do was learn to read. She also shared that he had begun helping her with her bills and business; needless to say, she was very pleased. The frosting on the cake came when, at the graduation ceremonies, he received the award for most improved student. As he stood up and raised his hands in the winner position, I was in the back mirroring his victory.

Another story from the same class involved a set of twin girls, both struggling to read and write. One in particular had quite a history of discipline issues, most of which had to do with fighting when other students made fun of her. She also was instructed as detailed in this book. She made rapid gains in reading and spelling, and her behavior issues dissipated. At one point, she asked her mother, "Where was Mrs. McGrew when we were in the first grade? She could have taught us then, and we could have learned a lot more." The last I heard, both girls had graduated from high school and enrolled in college, one with the aim to be a kindergarten teacher and the other, more outgoing one, to become a resource specialist and help students so they would not have to go through what she had.

Recently, I had the privilege of coaching an intern through the beginning phases of this process with a seventh-grade student whom everyone else had written off as a nonreader. The intern recognized that the young man was bright and articulate, and in fact he had learned a lot of coping skills to hide his inability to read. She commented that she would really like to help him. After she made the same comment two or three times, I asked her if she really meant what she said. Her reply was that she would do anything to help her student because she could see how much of his education he was missing. I told her it would not be easy and that it would take a lot of patience because there is no magic bullet—just direct instruction, practice, feedback, and patience. She was willing to give it a try, so together we proceeded through the process that is described in Chapter 5, which addresses teaching older students. When I finally got to meet and observe this young man, it was very obvious that he had a severe auditory processing deficit. The good news is that he made great progress—not fast, but good, steady progress—and you could not have found a more motivated student anywhere. He was in my intern's room every day after school. It was a joy to watch how proud he was that he could now spell and read some of the very basic consonant-vowel-consonant words that, up to this time, had eluded him. An added bonus came when the intern announced to me that she knew what she wanted to do with her career: "I just have a passion now that I understand how to teach reading so the students really get it. This is what I want to do."

That is the reason I took the time to write this book—so that I could share the passion and joy I felt when I was working with students, helping them develop the reading process, and at the same time building them up as learners and setting them on a firm road to their education.

# Introduction

This book is a guide to the best approaches for teaching the very beginning stages of reading and writing. It also includes ways to further develop the reading and writing processes as well as some strategies for developing study skills.

This book is intended to help teachers; it is one thing to know what students need and another to untangle the gobbledygook from what really works. Breaking the sound-symbol code is mandatory for learning to read because it is one of the three cueing systems. This book will help teachers, as well as parents, understand what their children need to become good readers. It is intended to help those who would teach reading understand some of the basic concepts that are needed for the reading and writing processes to develop along with some effective ways to teach them.

I did not write this book to address political and administrational problems within the education system. I wrote it to give parents and teachers the information they need for developing the reading and writing processes with their children.

I have organized the information into two distinct sections: a teaching manual which is this book and a materials manual which can be found on a CD. As you learn the sequence and techniques, the teaching manual (first section) will become a reference guide that will be needed only occasionally.

The materials manual on the CD is designed so that you can print out only the materials that promote the word and sound combinations that you are working on at the time. The information is available on CD. For ordering information, contact the author at the address below or mail $12.00 (check or money order) with your name and address to:

Louise McGrew
10654 Ave 104
Pixley CA 93256

# Chapter 1:   Facts about Reading

It is time for educators and parents to stop the pendulum! It's time for common sense to prevail and for children to be taught using research-based best practices with the most effective methods known.

The truth is that all reading programs have strengths as well as weaknesses, and while some students learn best using one technique, others achieve more success from alternative strategies. This means that most programs and methods have a place in the development of the reading process and, if they are used effectively, almost all students *can* learn to read.

**Fact:** Reading is as developmental as talking and walking. Timing is *everything*.

**Fact:** Phonics (the letter-sound correspondence) is one cueing system and needs to be taught through direct instruction, which means someone needs to explain and demonstrate how the letters and sounds work in the English language.

**Fact:** Syntax (the rules of language organization) is a cueing system and needs to be understood and used as the learner hears it modeled both in conversation and from the written word, as in stories.

**Fact:** Semantics (the meaning of language and context clues) is a cueing system and must be developed to make reading meaningful. Again, this is best done through conversation and lots of stories.

**Fact:** The majority of people, including our students, are visual learners.

**Fact:** There is a minority of students that needs extra auditory or kinesthetic strategies to access the sound-symbol relationships (mnemonic aids).

**Fact:** Approximately 80 percent of English words are phonetic.

**Fact:** Approximately 200 of the most-used words in the English language are not phonetic. (They must be taught by alternative methods.)

**Fact:** Discovering, making meaning from, and comprehending what is being read is part of the reading process—the reason for reading.

**Fact:** Children who are set up to fail will become failures, while children who are programmed to succeed will.

**Fact:** Reading can be taught in a positive way so that almost all students can learn to read with confidence and success.

**Fact:** Positive, direct instruction at the students' instructional level is absolutely critical if some students are going to become successful readers.

**Fact:** No single reading program takes into account all these facts ... because reading is not about programs; it is about a *process*.

I have sifted through many programs and selected the best techniques from each. I then incorporated those techniques to create a multifaceted learning approach and environment that promotes the reading process from many angles. Several strategies, as well as many techniques, will be described with examples demonstrating where and how they can be used effectively and efficiently in the development of the reading process. These have worked well for me for many years; however, you may find that you need to adjust the ideas to fit both your and your students' situations and needs.

## *Programs*

The truth is that most of the prepackaged reading programs sold by large publishers contain far more *stuff* than is necessary, and many of these extras actually distract from the reading process. More often than not, teachers experience overload and are not sure what really needs to be covered and what is just fluff. (You can't get through it all, that's for sure.) This confusion generally finds its way down to the students. Remember, too, that these high-dollar programs are very scripted and do not allow for the flexibility that a real classroom needs. As important as systematic and sequential direct instruction is, one must teach in such a way that children are set up for success and not considered to be at the remedial level within the first month of school. Good teaching will minimize the negative educational experiences and give children the opportunity to see themselves as learners, not as failures.

## *Developmental*

A very important key in teaching reading is to recognize and understand that, in part, *reading is developmental*. Just as we acknowledge that children can learn to walk and talk at any time within a range of a year and still be considered quite normal, the ability to learn to read varies in individuals and should be a factor in considering when and how reading and writing should be taught. It should also help teachers and parents remember to be patient and allow the children in their care the opportunity to develop the readiness skills they need to be successful and not overreact when a student does not exhibit the aptitude that other students may be showing when reading is first being introduced. We have little control over the speed at which a child develops, but we can control how learning opportunities are presented, as well as what is expected of our children.

This book is designed to guide parents and assist teachers with the task of assimilating and developing materials and books in such a way as to ensure reading success for all.

# Chapter 2:   Whole Language

## Explanation

The whole-language concept took the reading world by storm in the 1970s and 1980s. The main idea was to immerse students in good literature and give them a rich background of language, with the notion that reading and writing would follow. The whole-language movement in its purest form excluded the direct, systematic instruction of phonics. It is safe to say that some students did learn to read under the whole-language precepts. However, the theory fell out of favor when it was discovered that many students being taught with this method could not read or write well. So, as is often the case, everything about whole language was jettisoned, which means that some very important ideas were abandoned as well.

## Language as a Whole

One important aspect of the whole-language approach was the development of oral language. In order for reading to make sense, our children need to understand that words communicate meaning. That means the first step is to talk to children and then, as they are able, carry on conversations with them, helping them see the words take on meaning. Parents, from the time your children are in your arms, talk to them; they need to hear the sounds they will later need for speech when they begin imitating you. Then, as they begin making utterances, continue saying simple words back to them. Once they are able to say a word, incorporate the word into a simple sentence. For example, if your child points down and makes a sound, you say "down." Then, as the child develops, he or she may point down and say "down," at which point you would respond with, "Do you want down?" Or if your child points to a cat and makes a sound, you say "cat." When the child is able to point to the cat and say "cat," you respond with, "Yes, that is a cat." Never reprimand or correct the child because he or she didn't say "cat" the first time one came into view. Learning the language is developmental, and your job is to continually and conscientiously model the next level correctly.

The development of language is a continuous process that will be ongoing for many years. So with that in mind, learn to think "conversation" all day, every day. It isn't about quality time; it is about *all* the time. When you are cooking, cleaning, washing, driving, playing, etc., talk to your children about what you are doing or what they are seeing. These kinds of interactions stimulate vocabulary development and make language easy because it is within a context and has meaning. So parents, *talk* to your children.

Teachers, if you have some children in your room who are obviously unfamiliar with language and how it works, make sure you spend some time developing their language.

It can be as easy as taking a walk around the campus and pointing out various things and describing them. It will probably be necessary to spend time in the classroom describing and naming all the paraphernalia. It will also be important to remember to use simple sentences so the students can understand you and duplicate your speech later, as well as to give them an opportunity to learn the vocabulary of the classroom.

It is also essential that your students get to practice the language. That will require scheduling time for structured interactions as well as some scheduled spontaneous language practice. The structured time could be the time when you are instructing them. While you are having them draw or cut, you describe everything you want them to do while you arc modeling it for them. Then you have them repeat back to you what you are doing as you model it once again. Using words in context is very helpful for establishing vocabulary and developing language. Keep your sentences simple and correct.

Unstructured time, otherwise known as playtime, is also a great time for continuing the development of language. While the children are playing with blocks, you can simply comment, "Danny is building a tower with blocks" and "Sally is building a higher tower." Always be on the lookout for ways to incorporate language in your activities. Developing oral language helps children learn to communicate because they begin to experience the power of language. The better developed a child's language is, the easier the reading process is going to be.

## A Love for Books

Another concept the whole-language approach encouraged was instilling a love for books. Good literature is of paramount importance if the reading process is to get off the ground. Children need to know what reading is so it will be something they want to learn.

This is probably the easiest part of the reading process to implement because the only things required are good books and a reader. Reading daily to a child should begin at birth and continue for as long as it is pleasurable for those participating. Remember, the key word here is *pleasurable*; a child should love story time and anticipate it with excitement, even requesting extra reading time. Just a tiny word of caution—be sure that whoever is reading either really enjoys it or is an excellent actor because the child's experience with reading must be positive.

## Good Books

A whole-language approach requires good stories. There are many lists of good books that children should be exposed to, and they all have their purpose. The most important point to remember is that you, the reader, should enjoy the story also. That isn't to say you won't tire of a child's favorite book long before the child does (especially in the case of preschoolers and early primary children), but your initial and underlying feeling for the story must be positive and reflect a feeling of enjoyment because you want the reading experience to be pleasurable. You want the child or children in your care to love stories, books, and reading.

As a side note, there are some fun books that may not have made the Best Literature Award list but often have an appeal to children. Your goal is to get children jazzed and excited about books. You want them to think of reading as an adventure and something they want to do. If a less-than gold-medal-winner book is fun, the child enjoys it, and it helps to stimulate the desire to read, go for it.

## Book-Handling Skills

If read to, little ones will automatically obtain book-handling skills, such as knowing the front, back, top, and bottom and understanding that we read from left to right. They develop a sense of how to use a book just by observing a reader handling one and then mimicking the procedure. Page turning and general care are also things that very young readers will learn from exposure to readers and books. However, an occasional child may need some direct instruction or at least encouragement in the care and handling of books. If that is the case, do it as gently as possible but remain firm in your expectations of how books are to be treated. Your expectations will of course vary depending on the child's age.

In the classroom, because of the diversity of your students and the various skill levels with which they come to you, it is important that, as you read to them, you also talk to them about the front and back and the top and bottom of the book, about turning one page at a time, etc. As they get older, you might include discussions about who wrote or illustrated the book, again developing vocabulary. As they understand what writing means, you can introduce the word *author* and explain that the author is the person who wrote the book. You could then describe drawing in connection with illustrating. Any opportunity to develop vocabulary should be seized with enthusiasm.

## *Dialogue*

Another important aspect of the whole-language approach is the discussion or dialogue that stories and books can evoke. The child's age and the type of story will determine the content of the discussion. With the little tots who are just learning to speak, there is a lot of pointing and naming and sound making. For example, you point to a picture of a dog and ask, "What does the doggie say? Grrr! Bow–wow!" This is the beginning of language and reading.

For parents, this stage of the reading process simply involves reading and enjoying books with your children. As they get older, follow up with any questions or discussions that seem appropriate. Often, children ask the questions, and you will need to supply the answers or at least the dialogue that leads to the answer. Reading should be equated with an enjoyable conversation, the acquisition of language, and generally a good time.

Reading in these very early stages can also lay a very important foundation in the area of phonemic awareness. From the beginning, include nursery rhymes and other childhood jingles, chants, songs, and poems in the selections you read. Silly works well and can be a lot of fun. The intent is to help your child acquire an ear for rhymes, which, of course, lead to word families later. Do *not* fuss with word families now; that will come as the child learns to read. But the ability to hear words that sound alike can be very advantageous to beginning readers, so while you are reading for fun, be sure to include children's poetry, nursery rhymes, and the like.

## Teachers

Please know that your students will come to you with varying skills and levels of experience. The beginning introduction to reading basically involves the same things for you as it does for parents. You, the teacher, should be reading to your students throughout the day. Books should be a part of every classroom and used as tools for research and learning, but no matter how many books may be used during the day, be sure to take time to enjoy a couple of stories just for the fun of it. With older students, between eight and ten years old, start a chapter book that might be of special interest and read a chapter or two a day until you complete the book. But please do not shelve the wonderful, beautiful picture books! Continue to use them and encourage the students to enjoy picture books as long as possible. For one thing, many truly wonderful picture books need to be treasured by all ages, and many are appropriate through seventh and eighth grade. It's a shame to miss any of them. The pictures themselves evoke a lot of language and encourage vocabulary development if used appropriately. Pictures are important because they help set the context of the story, and for beginning readers that can be very helpful. Remember, you can have beginning readers in any grade.

Whole language is all about establishing a love for books, stories, and reading. If this is ingrained early on, the desire to read will fuel itself and practicing the reading process will come naturally, not be viewed as something to be avoided.

## Prediction and Comprehension

Allowing students time to predict or guess what will happen next begins early on within the context of predictable stories. Then the same idea of prediction can easily be applied to less predictable books where confirmation or adjustments may be necessary as one continues to read. A good reader is always thinking ahead and considering where the author might be going. This ability is learned very easily as children hear predictable stories, begin following the story line, and are given the opportunity to "guess" what is going to happen next. At first it may be on the second or third reading before they are confident enough to try a guess. That's fine, as that means their comprehension and memory are serving them well. It is fun to watch them "predict" during a story they have already memorized; they are so enthusiastic and excited as if they are hearing it for the first time. This is setting them up to succeed, and that is one of your main jobs throughout the teaching of the reading process. Be sure you are encouraging and supportive. Reading may not be new to you, but putting all these new concepts together is new to them, so help them enjoy it.

If you feel there is a need to begin developing comprehension at this time, retelling is a much better method of checking for understanding than asking comprehension questions. However, with older students, it may become appropriate to ask specific comprehension questions on occasion. Literature is the stepping stone from oral language to the language of textbooks, and it may be beneficial to occasionally pose comprehension questions. An excellent method of questioning is to cause the students to make connections between a previously read story, article, or real-life situation to what was just read. Reading is one of the great building blocks of critical thinking, and any additional development in this area can only be beneficial. For students, actually thinking through what they have just read and connecting it to something else in their knowledge bank requires more processing than just answering a question like, "How many buckets of cherries did the girls pick?"

## Literature Studies

Literature studies are recommended as part of the whole-language approach. There are as many ways to handle literature studies as there are teachers and classrooms. The studies should not wear out the story, but some stories lend themselves to more in-depth thought and consideration. Thinking through story lines and understanding the components of stories is a good way to develop an understanding of what makes a story interesting. Remember, too, that the students' ages and skill levels need to be considered when planning literature studies.

There are many approaches to reading chapter books as a class. Some teachers prefer to have students give a quick review of where the class left the story the last time they read together and then pick up and continue from there, without any documentation. Others like ongoing literature journals. There is no right or wrong way to read and enjoy a good book. The key is to enjoy the story. Remember that if children are going to become lifelong readers and learners, it must be something they enjoy doing. If you and your students get too bogged down in dissecting every line or writing volumes for every chapter, the chances are that some of the joy will be lost.

Literature studies and journals most certainly have a place in the classroom, but just enjoying a story for its own sake is important also. Just as variety is the spice of life, variety can help maintain interest in reading, so don't wear out one method.

## A Variation of Journal Writing?

One thing that can work well is to just pass out blank pieces of paper. For older students with whom you are reading a chapter book, a quick review of what happened in the previous reading is appropriate. For younger students, give them a little background for the story that is about to be read. Instruct the students to wait for a predetermined point in the story, where they will begin drawing a picture about the story while you continue reading. Sometimes you will choose what the students are to draw, and other times it is nice to let them choose. It may depend on what is being studied or if there is some particular importance to one aspect of the story. Some possible examples include the following:

- The most exciting part
- Their favorite part
- The setting/the characters
- The clues (if it is a mystery)
- What they can see based on the author's descriptions
- What the story is about
- The main ideas; the events that make up the story line

This particular technique does two special things. For older students who are struggling with print, it helps level the playing field a bit. More often than not, the less academic students enjoy stories but find writing about them to be laborious. However, they can draw, so their level of success is increased with this activity.

Just as a point of interest, often some of the more academically advanced students will get upset with the idea and will want to just write a summary. (Tell them you don't need a summary because you have just read it.) However, if they feel their drawings are inferior, making them self-conscious and a bit resistant to this exercise, require all the students to draw if they want credit for doing the assignment but give them the option of writing about what they drew so that their confidence remains intact. Once the students realize that it is not about art, they become fairly creative.

The real bonus for all the students is the development of their visualization skills. The words they hear become pictures, which transfers into visualizing what they read, which boosts their comprehension skills. Readers must be able to form some sort of picture or concept in their minds; that is, they need to link the words they hear and see to ideas so the words have meaning because it is then that comprehension can truly take place.

## Cartoon Strips

Cartoon strips can also be very useful in developing visualization and comprehension skills. To sequence the details of the story, one has to organize the events. This technique can be adapted to your students' ages. For younger students, two or three squares might be enough. The obvious choices for two squares would be drawing the beginning and the end. If you opt for a third square, the middle square might be their favorite part or the most exciting part. These cartoon strips can be drawn after you have read a story or while you are reading it. Children would, of course, have to wait until you started the story before they could begin drawing, but most stories, especially those for the younger students, get started on the first or second page. For older students, it could be an ongoing assignment so that by the time the book is finished, they have all the main events of the story sequenced and illustrated. The idea is that you want all the students to demonstrate comprehension, and this is a fairly painless way to allow them to do it. This technique allows for easy review and can lead the way to discussions about the story. For example, students could explain why they chose to draw what they did. Remember, there is no right or wrong drawing; for the most part, this would be a subjective exercise.

It is not necessary to have the blank cartoon strips made up in advance; the students, especially from first grade on, can draw their own boxes. But providing rulers would be helpful.

## Celebration

After a book is completed, whether it is a chapter book or a picture book, it is sometimes nice to celebrate it. Different books lend themselves to different activities. The completion of a chapter book may spark a need for a mini celebration as a class or family. Your imagination and time are probably the only limitations. Adding a bit of fun to finishing a chapter book or some other book of great significance increases the importance placed on books. Celebrating can be a great way to encourage reluctant readers. Just be sure to keep the celebrations in perspective. They should not become the reason for or the focus of reading. Good literature can stand alone; it's read because it's good to read.

Different stories lend themselves to different activities, such as the following:

- Cooking something that might have been served in the story
- Making some article of clothing that might have been worn
- Dressing up as a favorite character on a designated day
- Making a toy or tool from that time and place
- Playing a game that might have been played in the story
- Creating a poster that would sell the book
- Draw or paint murals of favorite parts or certain aspects of the story
- Writing a newspaper article about an event in the story
- Building a diorama
- Visiting the place where the story was set (or some place similar)
- Writing a letter to the author or one of the characters
- Writing a script for a scene from the story
- Designing a set or wardrobe for a scene in the story
- Rewriting the ending or writing a sequel
- Analyzing and presenting the sequence of or problems in the story

- Anything else you might be inspired to do to celebrate the story

Included in Section 12 of the Materials Manual are various approaches for as well as alternatives to book reports.

## Importance of Literature

Just as language is a developmental process, in which sounds and single words are the first steps toward communication, so it is with literature. Literature provides a very important step in moving from basic communication skills to success in school. Reading to children is important because it allows them to hear the written language, which helps them make the transition from everyday, conversational language embedded in the context of what you are doing together as a class to the language of literature and finally to the language of academia and informative texts. The language of stories is the all-important bridge between basic communication skills and success in reading and comprehending expository texts, which is necessary for success in school.

## Whole-Language Strategies

Some points to remember about whole-language strategies follow:

- Begin reading to children early on—the earlier the better. Perhaps your school can implement a community plan to encourage parents to read to their infants.

- Consider adopting a grandparent, aunt, or uncle to come into preschools and day-care centers as additional reading supporters.
- Pleasure reading or "reading just for fun" is where many important reading skills can be introduced. Begin listening for sounds, such as first sounds, last sounds, sounds that sound alike, and words that rhyme.
- Read daily, and allow children to see you read. Again, encourage parents of school-age children to read to their children and model reading in their homes.
- Read, read, read. Read to yourself. Read to your child. Read to your class. Just read.
- Reading for pleasure is the key to successful reading.
- Reading is the key to successful learning.
- Research is now revealing that the difference between a student in the eightieth percentile and one in the twentieth percentile is fifteen to twenty minutes of out-of-class reading every day.

**So again, READ, READ, READ!**

# Chapter 3: Phonemic Awareness and Phonics

This chapter is designed for those who are teaching students at the very beginning stages of the independent reading process, especially kindergarten and first grade. Children come to school expecting to learn to read, and teachers should not disappoint them. With that in mind, it is important to begin teaching letter recognition and letter names and sounds right from the beginning. It is absolutely crucial that you teach with an understanding of how vital these first lessons are to your students. You are handling a two-edged sword. In any given classroom, all the students need to learn the sound-symbol relationship; however, there may be several students who are not developmentally ready and some who have never seen print before and really have no idea what all the fuss is about. As the teacher, you must carefully scaffold your lessons so that every student can participate and learn with a feeling of success.

Key factors for good reading instruction include the following:

- Small groups
- Direct sequential systematic instruction
- Mnemonics
- Guided practice
- Instant positive feedback
- All concepts taught to mastery

At the risk of sounding melodramatic, for some of your students this very well may be their first experience with the reading process. How you present your lessons, how you measure success, how you reward your students, and how you correct their mistakes can most certainly make or break some of them. Remediation is no substitute for learning it right and being successful the first time.

Truly, this is a most crucial point in your students' academic lives because how well a student learns to read determines how well they will do academically and whether they will become an independent learner or one that struggles and fails throughout their education.

This, then, is the most important aspect of your job—balancing "what needs to be taught" with "who is ready." It really isn't quite as difficult as it sounds, but you must constantly and continually be cognizant of your students' needs.

### *Developing Letter Recognition*

In order to meet the needs of all your students as well as the requirements of state and district standards, you must adopt a two-pronged approach to your program. The first order of business is getting a *good* alphabet chart placed at their eye level. Sing or say an alphabet song every day while someone points to the letters. Some educators have a problem with some of the songs because they feel the names of the letters are not distinct enough. You determine what is best for you and yours. Just remember that all but five of the consonants (*w, h, y,* and the hard sounds of *c* and *g*) have some part of their sound in their name. So knowing, and knowing well, the names of the letters in the alphabet goes a long way toward beginning the reading process.

Keep the lessons and practice as low key as possible and work toward each of your students' mastering the names of the letters. Flash cards can be used in an appropriate manner for additional practice. Showing a flash card with a single letter and a picture to help cue the name of the letter to the entire class and having them respond in unison is a way to reinforce the name of the letter. As a word of caution, select the pictures carefully. Be sure the pictures relate to the names of the letters. In developing letter recognition, *do not* confuse the sounds with the names. It is not easy to keep the cute little alligator out of the mix, but know that there will be a place for him when we get to sounds. For this section, the names of the letters are the focus. That is to say, the name of the item in the picture should begin with the name of the letter, except of course for *w* and *h*. For these two, you just have to include a picture of a watch or a horse, or whatever you have that begins with those letters. Then for *c* and *g*, use pictures that represent their soft sounds because they are more closely connected to the names of the letters. The picture for *c* should be a city or a circus, while the picture for *g* would be a giraffe, a giant, or a gerbil. For the vowels, use pictures that represent their long sounds. For example, the picture for *a* should be an acorn, ape, or aphid; for *e*, it should be an easel, equator, or equipment. (And can you make it cute?) Everything will get sorted out as you teach the sounds in a controlled, systematic method. But for this part of the process, stick to the letter names.

Flash cards with only single letters can be used in the same manner as long as everyone is supported and feels successful. Anything that allows the students the opportunity to say or recognize the names of the letters is helpful.

## Games for Practice

A multitude of games are available for reinforcing these skills. Bingo is always a good game, and remember, homemade works as well as store-bought. Making up blank bingo cards and laminating them works well because then your students can use markers to fill in the blanks with the letters you have them working on. Then everything can be erased and used again later with the same or different letters, depending on what they are studying. A few other good standbys that can be adapted and are very effective are old maid, concentration, and go fish. Again, you may need to make your own cards with the alphabet and corresponding pictures. With these activities, you give the students the opportunity to recognize letters and say their names. Fluffy and fluttery are not what we are after. The truth is that too much fluff sometimes gets in the way of learning. When the game becomes the focus, the result is very little transfer of skills. Remember that the goal, the reason for doing any of this, is to jump-start the reading and writing processes.

## Clarification

As the teacher, you will be practicing and working with the entire alphabet at one time through chants, songs, charts, and games. This can be done with the entire class, except of course for some of the games, which are played in supervised centers.

At the same time, you will begin to introduce specific letters and their sounds and practice them out of sequence. This is discussed in detail later in this chapter. Teaching the sounds of the letters, or phonemic awareness as it is known in some circles, must be done in small groups so you can monitor your students very carefully. This is where the instant feedback is critical. Remember that everything that is done in the classroom is done with the idea of giving every child a positive learning experience and developing a learner's attitude.

## *Phonemic Awareness*

Besides knowing the names of the letters, another important component of phonemic awareness is speed. Not only do your students need to know the names of the letters, they need to be able to recognize them rapidly. The technical term for the speed of recognition is *automaticity*, which simply means that the student knows the names of the letters thoroughly and quickly. Now, as important as this is, *please* do not put yourself or your students through unnecessary stress. Work at this skill in a positive way. Start out with songs, chants, and games. Remember, it is important to set the students up for success. No matter what, do not allow the importance of this skill to get in the way of your students' needs. They *must* feel positive about what they are doing. The feeling of failure can destroy the desire to learn, while success leads to more success. Work at this steadily and gently, allowing for lots of practice and assistance. Learning takes time; it does not happen the first or second time you go over the letters.

My preferred technique for teaching the letter-sound relationship—one that has worked extremely well for both advanced students and for the less mature—is the Phonovisual Method. This method consists primarily of using two charts. It can be used simultaneously with the alphabet chart discussed previously that you use to teach the names of the letters. Do not worry about confusing the students because they are going to have to learn to recognize the letters in many different places and in different written forms anyway. Also, keep in mind that you are going to be there to monitor and assist throughout this learning process.

One easy way to teach this concept is to tell students that each letter has a name *and* a sound. It is not too difficult of a concept because most children understand that they have two names. So it is not much of a stretch for your students to sing the alphabet song while they begin learning the phonemes they will be using to read and write with for the rest of their lives.

By definition, a phoneme is the smallest unit of speech. It can be one letter such as *p*, two letters such as "th," or even three such as the "igh" in the long "i" spelling. Alphabet letters used singly and in combinations make up the written phonemes that we articulate through our speech and then use to spell what we read and write.

## Teaching Sounds Correctly

The need for visual discrimination is fairly obvious; students must be able to recognize the various letters. What is often overlooked is the importance of auditory discrimination. Auditory discrimination is even more crucial to learning to read than visual discrimination because students *must* be able to recognize the sounds that are produced when we speak. Reading, after all, is speech written down. This is very important to know as a teacher because it plays into the developmental aspect as well as possible areas of weakness. This means you will need to teach to the areas of strength with gestures and pictures while the auditory piece develops and the student becomes able to process all the sounds that make up the English language.

When you initially teach a sound, take a few minutes to explain and discuss how the sound is made in the mouth. With the voiceless consonants, explain that these sounds are made with air. The voice is not used; that's why they are voiceless. Have students hold their hands in front of their mouths when they make the sounds. Make sure they are making the sounds correctly and that they can feel the air exploding or escaping from their mouths.

Then, when you begin with the voiced consonants, explain that their mouths and tongues will be doing just what they were doing when students made the voiceless sounds, but now they will "turn on" their voices. Explanations and checking that each sound is made correctly as you introduce it is important. One wonderful benefit of this method is that it corrects a lot of "sloppy" speech and eliminates the need for special speech classes later. Discuss with the students what their lips are doing, where their tongues are, and what their tongues are doing. You will need to review this information periodically. Asking it as a question and letting the students explain is a good way to review but only after you have taught and reviewed the information and are sure the students are ready to verbalize it. Always be prepared to assist or review yet again, without any reprimands. Keep in mind that you have used this system a long time but it is a brand-new concept for your students. It is your job to make it comprehensible and usable.

## Consonants

Examples of the organizational charts for consonants and vowels are included in the Materials Manual, Section 1. They are very well organized and allow for the teaching of most of the basic spelling patterns and even some idiosyncrasies of the English language. There are four basic types of consonants: voiceless, voiced, nasal, and liquid. The voiceless consonants are made with only breath escaping or exploding from the mouth. An almost identical set of voiced consonants are made with the mouth, lips, and tongue making the same motions used to make the sounds for the voiceless consonants, except now the vocal cords vibrate, making the voiced consonants sound louder.

The nasal consonants are made up of three sounds and are basically produced through the nose. And the fourth group is called liquid, tongued, or slides because the mouth, especially the tongue, moves more in the making of these sounds.

The first column is the voiceless consonant phonemes, the second column contains the voiced consonants, the third column is the three nasal sounds, and finally the fourth column is the liquid phonemes. Please take special note of the first two columns and the positioning of the phonemes. These are set up as pairs because we make them exactly alike or so close to the same that confusion often occurs in pronunciations and spellings. (Example: for p- and b-, the lips and tongue do exactly the same thing, but p- uses only air—no voice—while b- includes the use of the vocal cords.)

Start with the voiceless phonemes, which are the most difficult to hear and therefore the most difficult to learn. With this method, what the student learns is continually repeated. The teacher adds to what has already been taught so the students are constantly reviewing all the sounds. By the time all the consonants have been taught, the students will have heard, seen, and written the difficult sounds many more times and will have mastered them along with the easier sounds.

As a special note of clarification, when reference is made to consonant sounds, it includes both the single consonant letter making one sound as well as the digraphs (two consonants representing one sound). Digraphs need to be taught in a matter-of-fact manner. When *s* and *h* are joined together, they have a special sound: sh-. This is how the letters are used in the written English language, so learning them correctly at the beginning as a complete unit of sound makes using the English spelling patterns easier later.

## Practice

To those of you who have been taught to run and hide when you hear the word *practice* or *drill*, they are not bad things. In fact, there are new mottoes among those in the know: "drill and skill," or even better, "drill and thrill." Children do want to learn, and they do get excited when they realize they've learned something new. Practice allows them to achieve high levels of success as they use their new skills. As you know, a great sense of pride arises when you know that you have learned something and can do it well.

You do not have to practice in exactly the same way every day, but the sounds that are learned need to be "exercised" continually so the students really get to know them. (This, by the way, pays off down the road as children begin to actually read; the quicker the sounds come, the less comprehension is lost.) Automaticity plays an important role in the reading process of an efficient reader, and it will only happen after the sounds become *very* familiar. The ability to read rapidly or fluently is one of the key indicators of a good reader. The less brain energy one expends on decoding, the more brain energy one has available for comprehension, which of course is the reason for reading.

## Phonemic Progression

A logical progression for teaching the letter-sound relationships will be discussed here. See Chapter 4, How to Teach Phonics and Beginning Reading. It discusses the how-to of direct instruction, guided practice, and instant feedback.

Begin by teaching the first five voiceless consonants because this allows for both written and oral practice as well as some gamelike activities: p-, wh-, f-, th-, t-. For kindergarteners, spend five to seven days practicing and using the letters and sounds, letting the students become very familiar with the shapes and sounds of these five letters. After that, add a new sound every third day or so, but continue using the original five. If you feel you are moving too fast for some of your students, one new sound a week is fine too. The progression is as follows: p-, wh-, f-, th-, t-, s-, sh-, ch-, k-, h-.

After working through the progression, determine whether the students have learned all the voiceless consonants and are using them with some degree of confidence. They should be able to locate the sounds on the chart, recognize them when they hear them, write them well enough to recognize them, and be comfortable with the concept of letters having sounds. Then you are ready to move to the next step in the process.

### First Vowel Sound: -ee-

Teach -ee- first. This is a wonderful, consistent vowel sound that allows the students to begin practicing with words. Remember to use -ee- only with letters the students have already learned and are currently practicing. Some examples are *peek, peep, feet, teeth, keep,* and *seek.* Begin the process of putting letters together and arriving at a word. The students usually catch on to the idea that there really is a purpose to this letter/sound thing and feel a real sense of accomplishment as they enter into the world of words. Now you will concentrate on the rest of the consonants until all the consonant phonemes have been taught. Again, see Chapter 4 for instruction and practice ideas. Lists of words and sentences are included in Section 8 of the Materials Manual. Once the students are on their way to mastering the -ee- with the voiceless consonants, then you and your students are ready to take the next step.

### Two Not-So-Constant Consonants

Offer students an additional bit of information to help eliminate some confusion in these beginning stages of learning the sounds: tell them that, for now, *c* and *g* will use only their hard sounds. That is, *c* will make the sound k- as in *cat,* and *g* will make the sound g- as in *goat.* Just for the record, *c* does not have a sound of its own. It borrows sounds from *k* and *s.* For now, though, do not bother the beginners with this information. Just teach *c* as "*k*'s helper" and *g* with its hard sound as shown on the chart.

## Voiced Consonants

The voiced consonants are b-, w-, v-, th-, d-, z-, j-, and g-.

Don't forget that you never stop exercising and using the voiceless consonants as you add the voiced consonants. So, along with *peep, feet,* etc., you work with *beep, deep, jeep, week,* and so forth. Review the charts in Section 1 of the Materials Manual.

Just because these letters and sounds, as well as the reading process itself, are so natural to many of us, we forget that they need to be taught and clarified for many of our students. The only difference between the voiceless and voiced consonants is the use of the voice, but this small difference causes a lot of misspellings. It is important to help students understand this phenomenon so they learn to listen carefully, speak clearly, write correctly, and read with confidence.

## Pairs

Be sure you take time to show your students how the pairs work—that is, how p- and b-, wh- and w-, f- and v-, th-(voiceless) and th- (voiced), t- and d-, s- and z-, ch- and j-, and k- and g- are made the same way in the mouth. The difference is in the use of the vocal cords. Students may not understand the first time you explain it, but eventually it will click for them because you are going to review the concept periodically, especially when someone confuses one sound in a pair for the other. Watch for students to write a *t* when they should have written a *d* (*weet* for *weed*). This is one of those teachable moments when the teacher explains the concept again and has everyone in the group feel their throats so they can identify the difference. There should be a tightening or a vibration when d- is spoken. When you review this concept, make sure it is not done in an incriminating way. *Never* make students feel as if they have failed by not remembering. There is a lot of information being presented, and for most of your students this is the first time they have worked with these concepts, so it is your job to reteach in such a way that the students learn in a positive manner. Even as adults, brand-new material doesn't always "go in" the first time we hear it. Just review and reteach with a smile!

## Another Spelling for -ee-: -ea-

Present this concept by saying, "This is how the English language works. Sometimes -ea- helps out, and when it does, it makes the same sound as the two *e*'s together." Do not confuse this spelling with the short -e- sound of the -ea- in *bread* and *head*.

When you're writing and modeling, it is no problem. When your students see -ea-, they will say -ee-. However, you will need to determine whether you want to hold them accountable for the -ea- spelling when you are dictating words and sentences to them. If in the beginning you allow them to just use the -ee- spelling, you can help them differentiate later or give them a verbal cue as well as a gesture to help them know when they need the -ea- spelling. Just so you know, whether you have them use the -ea- spelling now or later, you will need to give them a cue so they know which spelling to use. Remember, we are not memorizing a bunch of spelling patterns. We are working at mastering the sounds and the symbols that stand for those sounds. You will need to be a part of helping them know what letters to write.

When you dictate a word that requires the -ea- spelling, just say "*e* with a partner letter" and then hold your hand in a loose fist with your thumb sticking out like the tail of an *a*. That is all it usually takes. You may, however, need to teach them what *partner* means. Demonstrate the gesture so they know and understand what you are referring to when you cue them.

### Nasal Consonants

The three nasal sounds—m-, n-, and -ng—are the next phonemes in the sequence. It is important to note that -ng is never used at the beginning of a word. So although you will teach the -ng phoneme as one of the nasal consonants, you will not be able to incorporate it into words until you teach the short vowels. You can add *meet, need*, etc., to the list of practice words (see Section 8 of the Materials Manual).

### Liquid Consonants

Finish the consonant phoneme sequence by teaching the liquid consonants: qu-, l-, r-, y-, and -x, adding still more words, such as *queen, wheel,* and *green*. See the list in Section 8 for more.

That covers all the consonant phonemes in the English language with the exception of those consonants that don't follow the regular patterns or have unusual rules for use. Our beginning students do not need to be worried with those at this time because they are in the initial stages of reading and writing. Remember, we want to keep it simple and give the students a sense of confidence by working with the most consistent patterns first.

To reiterate, as you add new letters and sounds, *do not* stop working with the ones you have already taught. You will need to plan more time, but use and exercise what has been taught every day. What you are teaching must not only go into long-term memory, but it must be instantly retrievable, and that requires a lot of practice. Two important words to remember as you teach beginning skills are *model* and *mastery*. Teach what they need to know and allow them time to practice.

## Short Vowels

When most of your students are comfortable with all the consonant phonemes and -ee-, introduce the short -a- sound. You will immediately open up a cupboard full of words: *hat, cat, man, ran, path, and,* etc. Explain carefully how consonant-vowel-consonant (CVC) patterns make the vowel say its short vowel sound, or its "other name." Explain that when a consonant follows a vowel, it "chops off" its name and then the vowel can only make its sound.

## Progression for Teaching Short Vowels

Teach them in this order: -a-, -i-, -o-, -u-, -e-. The reason for this suggested progression is the usefulness of the vowels. The first few listed allow access to many more words than the last two, and -e- is really difficult to distinguish from the -i- sound. Some students hardly differentiate these sounds when they speak, so be prepared for some extra explanation and work. Even if they never really incorporate the sound into their conversational language, they can learn the difference between them. Learning to hear the difference between -e- and -i- and how to pronounce them correctly will help the students use the two appropriately when they read and spell. Listening, speaking, reading, and writing are all interrelated. The better they get at one, the better they will get at the others.

## Word Families

This is an appropriate time to introduce word families. As you progress through the short vowels, practice with the various word families is most appropriate. For example, teach *map, lap, cap* and *man, can, fan,* etc. Model and explain how easy the words are to spell and read because only one sound at a time changes. As always, allow for practice.

### -ck

It will be necessary at this point to explain that the -k sound is going to need help with the pesky short vowel sounds. Whenever the -k sound is heard after a short vowel, it will need the help of the letter *c*. That is, -ck will always be used immediately following a short vowel sound. This explanation, along with practice, takes care of when to use -ck and when to use -k. Note that the -ck combination is used only at the end of short vowel words, so model it, explain it, and give students ample opportunities to practice the concept. It is sometimes helpful to write a little -ck at the end of the short vowel line on the chart to give students a visual cue for when -ck is appropriate. Write it only after you have taught all the short vowels and are planning on practicing the concept. If you notice some of your students struggling with the -ck, you can practice the concept during your chart work, using -ack, -eck, -ick, -ock, and -uck. It provides a little variety and helps with the concept.

## Speed Bump

Do not rush through the short vowels! Allowing several weeks to teach each one is appropriate and necessary, especially for young students. You want those short vowel sounds to be cemented in each little brain. It is preferable to take an extra week or two rather than move too quickly. Learning the short vowel sounds is crucial to decoding longer words later. Multisyllabic words are composed of a lot of short vowel sounds, and the importance of learning the short vowels very thoroughly cannot be overemphasized.

For kindergarteners, this is really enough. However, occasionally you will have a few students who really want to learn more. If at all possible, distract them. Learning all the consonant phonemes and all of the short vowels is an admirable feat for kindergartners. Keep them busy reading, writing, and practicing what they know. Now is a good time to work on speed and fluency but not to the point of creating failure for any of your students. Keep it very positive. Everyone succeeds. It is also an appropriate time to add a few additional sight words—you know, the words that do not play by the rules. *Carefully* introduce one at time and let the students work with the new word while they continue to practice *all* the sounds you have taught.

## First Grade

As a teacher in an elementary school setting, the first

order of business when students return as first graders is offering a comprehensive review. It is necessary to make sure that students remember all the sounds that were taught. Take your time because extra time spent reviewing now eliminates confusion later. First graders should know all the consonant phonemes as well as -ee- and all the short vowel sounds.

If for some reason you have a few who don't know the consonants and short vowels, then you need to start at the beginning and be sure they learn these very basic concepts as quickly as possible in the most positive way. It is quite possible that you will need to set up a special group so that those students are able to receive the instruction they need to develop their reading process. *No*, you may not dump them into a group with students who have already mastered the basic concepts that were previously taught. Remediation does not look like failure if you as the teacher handle it in a positive way. It is much easier to teach the basic skills now rather than after the student struggles for several years, never understanding what the connection is between the letters, sounds, and words.

## *Diphthongs*

By teaching the diphthongs next, you allow the students additional time to further master the short vowels before they tackle the long vowels. If the long vowels are taught before the short vowels are learned to the level of automaticity, it can cause some confusion and be a bit of a problem. The spelling pattern may be where the issue lies as there is not much difference between CVC and CVCe. At any rate, experience has demonstrated that the more time you allow between the short vowels and the long vowels, the easier it is for the beginning students.

Once the consonants and short vowels are reviewed and firmly ingrained—that is, completely mastered and at the student's command—the next set of phonemes in the progression is the diphthongs. Diphthongs are two vowels together that have their own unique sound.

The easiest approach is to begin with the soft -oo- sound of *moon*. Then progress to the -oo- of *book*, -ow- and -ou- of *cow*, -oy and -oi- of *boy*, and the -or- of *fork* (officially not considered a diphthong but not an *r*-controlled vowel either, so for lack of a better spot, it's here). Offer additional information such as that -oi- is always in the middle of words and -oy comes at the end. These are all the diphthongs that include *o*.

Move to the "a" column and teach the -aw and -au- of *saw* and the -ar- of *car*. (Again, -ar- is not considered a diphthong, but it needs to be taught and fits well here.) The -aw or -au- sound is often very difficult for students because it sounds so much like the short -o- sound. This is especially true in the western states, where the only difference between the short -o- sound and the -aw sound is that -o- is only a tiny bit shorter than the -aw sound. So explain that the -o- is short and "cut off," while the -aw/-au- is a little longer and drawn out. When you say words with those two diphthongs, drag the sound out so the students can get used to hearing the difference between the short sound of -o- and the long, drawn-out sound of the diphthongs -aw and -au-. (Note that -au- will always be followed by a consonant.)

Dedicate at least a week or two to each diphthong sound or spelling, "showcasing" words with that sound and spelling pattern. Monitor your students; if they need more than a week or two, then give them more time. Mastering the sounds is what it is all about.

## *R*-Controlled Vowels

The next sound to teach is that of the *r*-controlled vowels. Be up front with your students and tell them that this r- sound is a major bother because there is no way of knowing which spelling is correct just by listening. Promise them some tricks, better known as mnemonic techniques, that will help them remember the more frequently used *r*-controlled words. See Chapter 6, A Potpourri of Ideas, for study techniques using mnemonic aids.

Because *r* controlling a vowel is a very difficult concept, it sometimes helps to tell the students that when *r* comes before the vowel, all the letters make their usual sounds, such as *rat, rug, rip,* etc. However, when *r* comes after the vowel, it sits on it and smashes the sound right out of the vowel. The vowel can't say anything, so no matter which vowel is there, it will make the -rr sound. The mnemonics will help them learn to spell these pesky words. Reading these words is actually no problem; when they see *r* after a vowel they read -rr, plain and simple.

## *When They Are Ready*

Up to this point, all the students will have worked fine together. In fact, that is one of the reasons this is such a good way to teach beginning reading. For those who are ready to read, it gives them the tools to do it. They start reading, and it is tough to keep up with them as they figure things out and move ahead on their own. For the less mature students who are not quite ready to read, this method lays the foundation for them. They can participate and do well with the scaffolding and support that you provide while they come to grips with one of the important cueing systems in the reading process. Then, when they do reach that all-important developmental level, watch out! They will be reading. Your previously immature students will be able to recognize letters. They know the sounds and how the sounds work together, so when the developmental piece comes together for them, they can read. No one had to fail; everyone has been successful the whole time. Actually, it's a rather amazing phenomenon. It's almost like a switch is thrown, and it all falls into place. The information has been learned and used, the maturation is attained, and the reading process moves ahead very quickly from this point forward, even for those who seemed to start off a little slow.

### Silent or Magic -e

Introducing silent -e or magic -e is a step of great magnitude. Do not take this step without some serious thought. This is one of the few times that special grouping could be considered because moving students out of the short vowels and the diphthongs before they are ready can be detrimental. It seems the short vowel sounds are more difficult to master, and they are also more difficult to revisit, or go back to, after the long vowels are introduced. To be the most effective, be sure you have taught the short vowels and the diphthongs to mastery before making the move to long vowel sounds. Be very cognizant of all of your students' skills and needs.

Remember that you will continue to practice and use all the phonemes—both the consonants and the vowels—daily for all your students. Be careful that you do not push your students into overload. If you are concerned about just one or two students because they are a little slower than the others, it might be better to let them move forward with the rest of your students. You do not want to single them out or make them look different. In such cases, you will need to be extra watchful and supportive, being there to give the correct responses and to be very positive in your feedback. Whatever you do, be sure that you continue to meet with all your students, constantly reinforcing and using what they have been taught.

It is of the utmost importance to watch for signs of maturation and readiness before teaching the ending -e. You must use your judgment.

### Teaching -e at the End

Once the consonants, the short vowels, and the diphthongs have been mastered, go for it and slip in the magic -e (also known as silent -e). You must explain very carefully that when -e shows up at the end of a word, the vowel in the middle gets to say its name. Again, you must know your students to determine whether you should do one vowel at a time or all of them at once.

For example, you can introduce -e's job and then share how it works with all the vowels: *mad, made; Tim, time; tot, tote; pet, Pete; dud, dude.* Or you can just demonstrate with one long vowel at a time and stick to it, such as *make, bake, tame, pale,* etc. It has been effective both ways with different groups.

One practical way is to demonstrate how -e works for all the vowels; the pattern CVCe, with the *e* at the end, requires a long vowel sound. That is, the vowel between the consonants gets to say its name if -e is tacked on to the end of the word. Then spend a week or so with each individual long vowel: *make, bake, tame, same, male, bale, pale*. Then add "i-e." Give the students time to become familiar with the various word families using that long vowel: *take, bake, cake*. Then practice with another set: *bike, hike, like, time, mine*. Finally, put all the long vowel words using -e together with the short vowel words that you continued to use as you were learning the long vowel words, and practice, practice, practice. See the vowel chart in Section 1 of the Materials Manual. Also, a list of sentences using long vowel words is included in Section 9 of the manual.

## *Double Duty*

Once the magic -e or the silent -e concept is grasped and fully understood, you are ready to present the double vowels. The age-old and almost always reliable rule is, "When two vowels go walking, the first one does the talking." Explain that *e* is so busy with so many jobs that the other vowels have to help out: *bail, pail, boat, goat*, etc. Again, it is important that you teach the concept of two vowels but that you then practice one vowel duo at a time. Work on the -ai- for a few days and then move on to the -ea-, which you may have already snuck in.

With -ai- and -oa-, just tell students that the vowels appear "with a partner letter," and that is usually sufficient. But if you feel a little more is necessary, then while you are saying the long sound of -a, hold up your little pinky, making it look like an -i. Then, when you say the long -o sound, make your hand into a fist with the knuckles down and the thumb sticking out like the tail of the *a*.

Then, it is on to the others, which include the three-lettered "i," -igh. When you teach the three-lettered "i," just tell students that this is how it is spelled and give them some sort of clue to help them remember it. Saying "three-letter i" and holding up three fingers is helpful. A few days with the -igh word family will make it theirs.

Some teachers refer to these as vowel digraphs, while others consider them alternative spellings for long vowels. It can become a game of semantics and has very little to do with the reading and writing processes, so teach the concept carefully and do not stress over what to call it. It might be helpful if all the teachers at your school site decided on the same term so that as the students move from one teacher to another, the terminology will remain the same. But in the end it is not really a big deal as long as the students master the concept.

### *Not Quite Constant*

Two consonants that are not always constant are *c* and *g*. The letter *c* has virtually no sound of its own; it borrows from *k* and *s*. The hard sound of *c* is the k- sound and can be made either alone or in conjunction with k-. While *g* makes its own distinctive g- sound, it also has occasion to borrow the soft sound of *j*. The rule is demonstrated below.

- *c* = s- when it is followed by *e*, *i*, or *y* (cereal, city, lacy)
- *g* = j- when it is followed by *e*, *i*, or *y* (judge, giant, gym)

Model, teach, and practice. If you have given students enough time to master the hard sounds, these will come easily with practice.

## Compound Words

Compound words are fun because they are made up of two smaller, known words, and they come out looking very long and important. They give the students a sense of achievement. So as they fit in to what you are teaching, use them as another way to bolster your students' sense of accomplishment. Use the techniques that have already worked, demonstrate them in your own writing, and then introduce them to your students along with an explanation of why they are called compound words. See Section 8 of the Materials Manual.

## Homonyms

It is necessary at this juncture to teach homonyms so students grasp the reason for the different spellings of words that sound the same. See Chapter 6, A Potpourri of Ideas, for mnemonic aids to help teach these concepts. Write *sail* and *sale*, *pail* and *pale*, and *mail* and *male* as pairs on a white board. Draw pictures to help your students visualize the differences between the two words. Discuss the idea that some words sound alike but are spelled differently and mean completely different things. Mini vocabulary lessons explaining the differences of the words' spelling patterns and their meanings are very helpful to the beginner. Again, take it slowly. Give your students as much time as they need to *master* the long vowels while you continue to review the short vowels. You want the students to be very comfortable and in control of the graphic-phonemic system, so be sure they thoroughly understand and practice it every day.

## Sometimes -y and -w

Some other long vowel spellings include the sometimes-*y*

and sometimes-*w* as vowels. *W* always appears in tandem with another vowel, so the students will be used to seeing it as part of two of the diphthongs. (Do not explain *y* and *w* until it is necessary, which it is after you have introduced the alternative spellings for the long vowel sounds.) Explain that *y* at the end of a single-syllable word (short word) makes the long -i sound (examples: *my, why, shy*) except when it follows *a*. When it does, it merely supports *a* so that *a* can make its long sound, such as in *may, stay,* and *pray*. But when *y* comes at the end of a two-syllable (long) word, it says the -ee- sound (examples: *penny, puppy, merry*).

Remind students that -ow also makes the sound in *cow,* and then continue on with -ow making the long -o sound. Don't forget that *w* teamed with *e* (-ew) steals the sound of *u* altogether. Almost always, -w is going to be at the end of a word, not in the middle, unless there is a suffix added to the root (base) word. For example, *grow, show,* and *stew* would become *growing, showing,* and *stewing*.

### Yet Another Vowel Sound

At some point, you will also need to deal with -ea- making the short -e- sound. If you wait until the short vowels and the diphthongs are mastered, it usually is not a big problem. Just explain that it is yet another idiosyncrasy of the English language, and as always, introduce it by modeling it first and then explaining it and using it. It really is not used that often, but *bread* and *head* are common words that students need to know.

### Consternation with Schwa

Every vowel sound sometimes makes what is known as the *schwa* sound. It is a difficult sound because, like the *r*-controlled sounds, there is no way to know the correct spelling just by hearing the word. That is why it is the very last sound to be taught. Telling the students that all the vowels get tired and lazy and sometimes make a "grunt" sound at one time or another makes them aware of it. As your students become more familiar with the language, they will figure it out. In the meantime, fudge a little in your pronunciations and give them cues for the words that have the schwa sound. For example, with *banana*, pronounce the first syllable with the short -a sound just like you pronounce the other two syllables. Your students will laugh, but they will appreciate the help you are giving them. Usually by this time, the exceptions and the bothersome sounds do not upset the students because they have a pretty firm grasp on all the regular players. This is especially true if you downplay the concept as one of those crazy things about the English language and, of course, help them out with a hint or two when needed.

## Just a Reminder

Remember that each concept needs to be taught through modeling, direct instruction, practice, and instant feedback. Often it is easier to teach if you expose students to a concept before you actually instruct them about it. As you will remember from the time you began teaching the consonants and -ee-, the main strategy was dictation. It is very important for students to hear the sounds and the language; it is after all what we want them to learn. Almost anything you want to teach about the English language can be taught very effectively through dictation. It is an efficient way to put into place all the *best* teaching strategies (small groups, direct instruction, modeling, practice, and instant feedback) while the students have the opportunity to hear and see what they are supposed to be learning.

Teach only one spelling at a time and allow time to practice before moving on to the next alternative or irregular spelling. *Hint*: Keep your chart up and refer to it as often as necessary. See additional tips in Chapter 6, A Potpourri of Ideas.

## Close Counts

Once the students have confidence in the graphic-phonemic cueing system, they will happily attack any word. The English language is such that getting close counts. Pronunciation attempts can get the students close enough that the correct pronunciation of the word will come quickly and easily if the students have been exposed to enough language and vocabulary to understand what word would make sense or sound right in that context.

## Controlled Reading and Writing

One point that cannot be stressed enough is that while the students are working their way through this very sequentially organized method of instruction, it is of paramount importance for them to use or exercise daily what you have taught. You need to monitor with great care what they are expected to read and write. The students are to be held accountable only for what you have taught. You do not want any confusion or frustration to interfere as they begin grappling with this coded system.

This is often referred to as controlled reading and writing, and there are those who are opposed to it. However, for a student's first encounter with twenty-six letters and upwards of forty-something sounds, it is important to keep what we expect of them manageable. It is not fair to expect them to learn the whole kit and caboodle at one time.

That does not mean you have to stifle creativity. If they are reading and come to a word they don't know and that falls outside of what has been taught, just tell them what it is. By the same token, if they are trying to write something, *do not* make them guess. Reading and writing are not guessing games. If it is a word they should know (all the sounds have been introduced), then help them listen for the first sound, second sound, etc. However, if it is a word containing a sound that has not been introduced, spell it for them and let it go unless they ask a question. Then it is important to answer honestly. Sometimes the best and easiest answer is, "This word doesn't play fair, and we will learn more about it later."

## Confidence

What you really want to focus on initially is what is constant. *Keep it simple.* Give the beginners some faith in the system. Help them see that the letters and the sounds do work together. There will be plenty of time later for the exceptions. The bottom line here is to give the students a real handle on the graphic-phonemic cueing system and—maybe even more important—confidence. You want them to know that they know the code and that they are mastering the system. And that, my fellow teachers, is what phonics is all about. With the decoding and encoding of print, the initial reading and writing process has begun, and the enjoyment and the learning can continue to be developed.

# Chapter 4:   How to Teach Phonics and Beginning Reading

In Chapter 3, Phonemic Awareness and Phonics, we primarily discussed the most appropriate progression for teaching the graphic-phonemic system. In this chapter, we will discuss how to implement teaching the phonics needed for reading and writing.

## Supplies

You will need two phonics wall charts—one for the consonants and one for the vowels. The Phonovisual Method is the author's choice (see Section 1 of the Materials Manual for the Organization of Consonants and Vowels). You will also need lined and plain paper, pencils, crayons, some single picture cards (optional but nice), magazine pictures (mounted and laminated if possible; clear contact paper works well also), white or chalk boards—a large one for the teacher and the small individualized size for the students—and eventually some books that you have reviewed to support what you are teaching.

## *Grouping*

For maximum teaching and learning to take place, you should work with groups of four to five students at a time. There is a lot of discussion currently on heterogeneous or homogeneous grouping, inclusion or exclusion, etc., but quite frankly the only variable that really seems to make a difference is the number. Keep the numbers such that you can monitor every student carefully. You want the students to learn every letter and sound correctly the first time so there is no confusion and nothing has to be unlearned later. Instant feedback is a key element in this approach to teaching reading. You do not want your students practicing anything incorrectly. Be there to help make corrections and give explanations when they are needed. If it is necessary, you take the blame when a mistake is made by saying something like, "I must not have said that sound clearly enough. Let me say it again." As the teacher, you are establishing a safe, fail-free zone. Students must become comfortable enough to take risks if they are to become successful learners.

## *Teaching Strategies to Consider*

It is important to note that some students will need supplemental information to thoroughly process new information. Chapter 6, A Potpourri of Ideas, lists many mnemonic strategies that are very helpful for learning new information. For the beginning reader, the two most helpful at this stage would be gestures and storytelling. Further examples are in Section 2 of the Materials Manual.

### *Chart Work: Always the Opening Exercise*

To begin, point to the letter *p* and say its name and its sound—"*p* says p-." Be careful to limit the p- sound so it doesn't come out as "puh." You do not want a vowel sound associated with the consonant sound. If you are using a wall chart, ask the students what the picture is, and their answer will be "pig." Ask, "What's the first sound you hear when you say *pig?*" Don't be too surprised if you hear someone say "g." The residual effect causes the last sound heard to still be in their minds. Just have them listen while you say the word, and then have them say it again until the majority *claim* they hear *p*. Repeat this process with "wh" and *wheel*, "f" and *fan*, "th" and *three*, and "t" and *top*. Now point to each picture and say the name of the picture, and then point to each phoneme and say its name and the sound it makes. For the first few lessons, you will need to repeat this procedure two or three times and maybe more. Remember that although you already know this, it is new to the little beginners.

Some may not need quite as much review and practice as others, but the "quicker" ones will tolerate it at this age and it does a world of good for the ones who need it. After a few lessons, fewer repetitions are necessary; reviewing the names of the pictures, the letters' names, and their sounds is usually enough. But always be ready to back up and repeat, taking extra care to pronounce the sounds correctly.

As you add new sounds, give them the same amount of introduction time as you gave the first sounds. You should constantly be checking for the correct pronunciation of each sound. Monitor and model where the tongue is and what the parts of the mouth are supposed to be doing.

This procedure should be rehearsed every day. Once students have mastered the sounds, then you can provide a one-time-through review. This chart review serves as a way to bring the sounds into the students' short-term memory banks for current use and is also necessary to help them establish the sounds in their long-term memories with one more practice.

## *Single Pictures*

After you have completed the chart work, pull out your single picture cards. Keep them in the order of the letters on the chart. Remember, provide stability and predictability—no tricks! You should have five cards, one for each sound, for your first lesson. Whether you have made them or bought them is of no matter. First, show the pictures: pencil, whistle, finger, thimble, table, or whatever your particular set of pictures includes. As you show the card, have students say the name of the picture. If you have been able to obtain two sets of cards, show the pictures in the same order as you did the first set. Carefully pronounce the name of each picture: pan, whiskers, flower, thistle, top, for example. This is simply extra practice, and the more the students hear the sounds correctly, the better.

*Note*: Depending on where your students live, their preschool experiences, and their home environments, you may find that mini vocabulary lessons are in order. You can use additional pictures, discussions, or paraphernalia to help clarify the meanings of words. These lessons help broaden the students' vocabulary base and expand their background experiences. And all the while, they will be hearing the sounds you are teaching.

This little routine of going through the card stacks takes only a few minutes and helps bring the sounds and letters into even clearer focus. After the first few weeks, as new sounds are being introduced, new pictures will be added as well. To add a great deal of fun and excitement (almost too much, with some groups), as the cards are being flashed, flip through the known ones fairly quickly (they know them) and then slow down or even stop as you come up on the *new* one. Look expectant, widen your eyes, and pretend to peek at it. It will be too much for the students. They will have to guess. At first, their guesses will be very random, but soon they will figure out that a new sound means a new picture that uses that new sound, and their guessing will become much more selective. At any rate, the element of surprise gives the oral repetition a whole new dimension. Also, developing the process of thinking and predicting serves the students well later in their reading process. Besides, it is fun!

In Section 3 of the Materials Manual, I have included Consonants in Context. They are little jingles that spotlight each of the individual sounds and use a lot of alliteration. The students have fun trying to repeat some of them as they almost sound like tongue twisters. The rhymes generally tickle their ears and add a little extra fun while they are learning to discriminate sounds. They are probably most effective when you are introducing the sound. They help add excitement to the introduction of new sounds and further enhance the idea that this whole letter/sound thing is special. Having the students listen for how many times they hear the sound also generates a little fun. They rarely miss a sound. Be sure you help with a little extra emphasis on the sound they are learning.

## Follow-Up Activities

Follow-up activities might help ingrain the lessons. Spread out many old magazine pictures, preferably mounted on heavier paper and laminated, about which students tend to get excited. Initially, you will need to discuss the pictures with the students. Ask, "What do you see that starts with *p*?" Continue with "wh," "f," "th," "t," etc. You will say only one sound at a time, of course, and be sure there is at least one picture showing something that begins with the sound you dictate. Your pictures may also lead to mini vocabulary lessons while you discuss various pictures and what is happening in them; sometimes you will need to give the students names for items in the pictures. When your students have learned enough words with the sounds you are teaching, then they are ready for the game. Take the pictures out, spread them on the table, and then say a sound that has been introduced and practiced. It's up to you whether they raise their hands, slap a picture, or grab a picture. All three ways work. It really depends on how rambunctious your students are and how much excitement you can stand.

As they develop an understanding of the game, try to work in a little language development along with the phonemic awareness and encourage complete sentences. For instance, a "wh" answer might be, "Wheel! This bike has two wheels." This game also allows for creative thinking. A picture of a sailing ship out at sea once elicited, "Whale! There's a whale under the ship on the bottom of the ocean." Then there was one answer for "th." The picture was of three kids in a pool and a full view of a house in the background. The response was, "Thimble! There's a thimble in the house." All are correct and well done. What you want to hear from your students is a word with the initial sound that you pronounced. The logic and creativity are extra.

Now you will need to decide about keeping score. It makes for more of a game, and a little competition does help to keep everyone on their toes. The best advice is to go with what you know of your students. It's important to strike a balance. Your goal is to help all of your students master the system. The connection between the sounds and the letters is what this is all about. So keep an eye on the very aggressive and the easily intimidated. It may be necessary to overlook the hand that's always up and to call on the hand that's never raised (when you're very sure they know the answer). Perhaps a little prompting is in order. It's very important for *all* the students that everything be positive and upbeat.

### *Tactile or Touch*

Another extra activity is texture writing. This is fun for everyone, but it does require time you may not have. A compromise might be using it once a week or only for the introduction of letters. It's necessary for you to determine your students' needs. For the record, it really isn't necessary for most students, but again, for those who need the extra input, the tactile or touch approach can make a difference in the initial learning process. Science tells us that there are more nerve endings in the ends of our index fingers than anywhere else on our bodies, so the idea is to put them to work.

You can use trays, burner covers, or shoe-box lids partially filled with sand or corn meal (If mice are a problem, corn meal is not a good idea. Salt can also be a problem for any one who has an open sore because with just a little bit of moisture, there will be tears.) Frankly, clean, dry sand is the best.

Some other good materials students can use for tracing letters and words are sandpaper, burlap sacking or any rough material, denim on their jeans, tree bark, rocks or bricks, or any other surface that will give those nerve endings a little extra excitement. Blocks with raised letters or letters precut from material or cards with the letters in glitter-glue, gel (put gel in sealed plastic bags), students' own forearms, and a few strips of fake fur or velvet might be fun for a change. Soft is nice, but it doesn't seem to have as much effect on the learning process as a somewhat rougher surface. But a little fun never hurt any process. You might even have some older students or parents come in to supervise the younger students making the letters with clay or dough. The possibilities are limitless.

Give the sound or the word and have the students write it on or in the chosen material. Students should say the letters' sounds as they write them. If it is a word, the students should sound out the word as they write it and then say the word when they finish.

## *Air Writing*

This technique has been used favorably by many and is considered to help not only with the reading process but also with developing handwriting. If you choose to use this technique, this is important: *big* is what counts. In order to be effective, the students must move their entire arms. Yes, you want to include shoulder movement as the students "write in the air." This is a very cost-effective technique because all you need are your students and enough space for them to make large movements with one arm without bumping into each other. This large muscle movement aids in coordination and seems to transfer to the fine motor skills as well. It is a technique that doesn't cost anything to try and, for some of your students, could make a big difference. However, it is not magic, and results are not seen in one or two sessions. If you feel your students might benefit from it, then give it a chance by using it every day for several weeks so you can make an accurate judgment as to whether or not it is effective.

## Work Sheets and Independent Work

In dealing with work sheets, a few cautions should be considered:

- The worksheets should not take the place of the interaction between the student and the teacher.
- Before the worksheet is considered complete, it should be 100 percent correct.
- Never mark anything wrong or erase anything until you or an assistant have asked the student to name what he or she called the picture in the first place.
- Make every effort to have the learners supervised so they practice correctly. Unlearning an error is more difficult than just learning it correctly in the first place.

For example, you may be expecting students to practice words beginning with the p- sound, but you find that one of your students has written a *b*. When questioned, the student calls the pail a "bucket." Okay, very good; it's correct. Depending on the student, you may or may not want to explain that another word for *bucket* is *pail* and that both are correct. Always ask your students about a questionable answer; there may be a reason behind it. Then, if appropriate (and/or necessary), explain the *other* correct answer. If you decide to leave the student's answer, write in what the student called it or a brief explanation so anyone else who might happen to see it will not think it has gone uncorrected.

No matter what activity or strategy you are using or from what point of reference your students may be working, the goal of every activity is to support and encourage the students. You want all of your students to view reading and writing in a positive, predictable way. When they pick up a pencil or a book, you want them to feel good, not defeated. That's why, no matter how many tries it takes, every student gets every answer right. Just like the little train, you want them to keep trying with the attitude, "I think I can."

## *Discipline*

Usually, there's very little in the way of discipline problems; however, should a difficulty occur, deal with it quickly. Perhaps a brief warning and *the look* will suffice the first time, followed by removal from the group the second time.

Establish the following early on:

- This time is very important, not a time for nonsense.
- This is fun, but there are boundaries.
- Everyone has the right to learn, and no one will be permitted to interfere with someone else's learning.
- Only the teacher makes corrections.

I never had to remove a student from a group. There was always too much going on, and no one wanted to miss out on the fun and the stories. Occasionally it is necessary to redirect to help some students stay on task, but generally there is so much interaction and everyone is so busy that there really isn't time for naughtiness.

One crucial element is that your students trust you and that they can feel your sense of care and concern for each of them. Your proximity and positive attitude toward them will carry your groups a long way. It is a very rare child who does not respond to positive, caring instruction.

When students make mistakes, take the blame if necessary. Say, "Maybe I didn't say it clearly enough. Let me say it again." Keep their stress level down; they will learn more if they feel comfortable and supported. Your goal is to lay the foundation for one of the cueing systems for the reading process while creating an environment where all the students feel safe. Participation is always rewarded with praise and positive responses. The *only* time rewards or positive feedback are withheld is when a student exhibits disruptive behavior. It just does not happen often because the peer pressure is great and it is the special time of the day that no one wants spoiled.

It is important to maintain a good sense of humor. Occasionally, teachers let the stress of their own lives— whether it be professional or personal—interfere with how they respond to their students. Although life can be stressful, it is important that we as teachers leave the negative feelings outside the classroom and focus on our students in a positive way. Sometimes, for some of those little annoying things that students can think to do, a laugh, a raised eyebrow, or a hand on the hip with an "Okay, what's going on?" look is quite sufficient. As often as not, students really just want to be sure you notice them. So one of the keys to discipline is to acknowledge your students as they join you for the lesson and make sure you are giving them positive feedback on a very regular basis. It will not take long for you to figure out who the really needy ones are, and then do your best to give them the positive attention they need without neglecting your other students.

## Second-Language Learners

Second-language learners may be very quiet during oral response time. Do not become alarmed. They are listening, and they are learning. At some point, they will surprise you. When you are doing oral responses as a group, watch to be sure they are shaping their lips and mouths correctly. It is okay to encourage, but do not push. They very well may be in the pre-emergent stage, where listening *is* the important part of their learning. Give them time and perhaps plan some activities in which they can respond by pointing. For example, have individual work sheets with all the working sounds printed on them. As you say words, they can point to or cover with their hands the correct response for the first sound they heard. Or perhaps when you play the magazine picture game, have them point to an object beginning with the sound you pronounced, and then you say the name of the object. English language learners (ELL) understand much more than they are comfortable trying to say. Keep the stress at a minimum. Let them listen and learn, and keep everyone working together toward the goal.

## Listening

This next activity is a listening activity, but for whatever reason students usually identify it as a spelling test. What it is, in fact, is an opportunity for the students to respond in written form to the sounds they hear. Please remember that in this exercise it is imperative that everyone gets a 100. One reason for the small groups is that you can monitor carefully what the students are doing. Instant feedback is crucial to good teaching. If a student writes a letter incorrectly (you said "t" and the student wrote "d,"), quickly erase the letter and have the student watch your mouth as you pronounce the sound again. Repeat if necessary. If the student is having a tough day, you may need to point to the letter on the chart while repeating the correct sound. Remember that your goal is to reinforce the connection between the sounds and the letters. You want the students to feel positive about themselves, so when everyone is done, everyone should have a 100. If you stamp papers with fragrant ink or give stickers or praise, everyone is a winner. There will be time enough for grades. Confidence is half of this game, and you must make the students believe in themselves and the system.

It is necessary to create an environment in which all the students feel safe and are willing to take risks. If they are afraid to participate, they will not develop the skills they need to become successful readers and learners. You, as the teacher, are setting them up to *succeed!* If they don't know it, it's because you haven't taught it to them. Remember, when someone is learning something for the very first time, it has to be presented and practiced many times before it is learned. This means you get to teach it until they learn it.

Initially, the students will write only the first sound they hear when you pronounce words. For example, if you say "wheel," the students write "wh"; if you say "tiger," the students write "t." Use words that are especially interesting or fun for the students because they are responsible for only the initial consonant sound anyway. Some fun words are *popcorn, peanuts, whiskers, whistle, fantastic,* and *fabulous.*

The younger students love big words. For this exercise, big words are fun. This exercise is useful when you are working with initial or final sounds. If you are practicing listening for the last sound, you might pronounce *elephant*. The students would write "t." When you feel your students are comfortable with the initial and final sounds, then they can practice them together. Be careful to select words that have sounds at the beginning and end that you have taught. Remember, no tricks and no surprises. As always, monitor your students. Frustration is not part of the process. If you have introduced all the voiceless consonants, you might give the word *fastidious*. The students would write "f—s." Or give *titanic,* and the students would write "t—k." Yes, "t—k" because we are talking *sounds,* not spelling, and the last sound is the -k sound.

## Real Words

Once the vowel sound -ee- is introduced, the students can begin writing complete words as you dictate them. Be sure to keep within the bounds of what has been taught. This does not mean you have to stop playing with the big words, though. Listening for just first and last sounds is still appropriate. It simply means you have two ways of practicing the discrimination of sounds, and both are valid and useful.

At first, alternate between the two and then gradually use the whole words exclusively for dictation unless you just need a change. It is through this exercise that students begin to develop an understanding about how letters work together to make words. The key here is for the teacher to pronounce the words very carefully and repeat them as often as necessary. Refer to the progression list to help you decide when to teach each phoneme; it can be found in the Teaching Manual in Chapter 3, Phonemic Awareness and Phonics, and in the Materials Manual, Section 4, Progression of Study. Additional words to use for dictation can be found in the Materials Manual, Section 8.

Again, the students may pick up on the idea of a spelling test. It is *not* a spelling test, nor is it a trick in any way. You are dealing with what has been taught, and this is an exercise to further imprint the sound-symbol relationship. A variation of this is to have an individual chalkboard or white board for each student. The white boards are relatively inexpensive. Discount home supply stores sell all white bath and shower paneling, which can be cut into smaller sizes, and old socks are great erasers. The students love the variety, and corrections are a breeze.

### More Pictures

This time, start with blank paper except for one phoneme on the bottom or top. With pencils or crayons, the students draw some things that begin with the designated sound. For example, if -p- is on the paper, students might draw anything from pennies to panthers or pies. The idea is that they tell you what they have drawn and you write its name. Two important things are involved: first, the students have to make the connection with words they already know and the initial sounds you are teaching them, and second, as they see you write the words for their pictures, they begin to understand the connection between objects and their written names. This is a beginning step for abstract ideas and is necessary for developing higher levels of thinking.

For any students who may have difficulty thinking of words, be there and help them out by suggesting some things they can draw. You can try asking questions that might trigger a correct response, such as, "What's the first sound you hear when you say Tony's name?" or "Remember the picture of the farm? What was the little boy feeding?" Or try, "What were you and Joe playing with at recess?"

## Blending

After the students have been introduced to the voiceless consonants and -ee-, write *sheep* slowly on the teacher's big board, saying the phonemes as you write it, and then end by saying the word *sheep*. Have the students say it as you run your hand under it, giving them the idea that the sounds all blend and run together. As consonant sounds are added, words are added as well.

Our goal is to attack the graphic-phonemic system from every possible direction: see the letters, hear their sounds, write the letters, say the sounds. This technique puts the hearing, seeing, writing, and saying together, and it helps the students develop a sense of "putting the sounds together," otherwise known as sounding out or blending. After you have repeatedly modeled this blending process, your students will become proficient at blending the phonemes into words.

The next step is to write several words slowly and carefully, saying the words as you are writing them. When you have completed at least as many words as there are students in the group, everyone reads the words together as a review and then the students can try them independently, with you prepared to lend support and encouragement. For some students, it may be necessary for you to "sound out" most of it with them. That's okay; we are just getting started in this process. In the beginning stage, it's very beneficial for the students to hear someone else while they are sounding out words or sentences. It may be that a double sensory connection—visual and auditory working simultaneously—helps some students. At any rate, once the word has been sounded out, it is then pronounced normally and the student gets to erase the word.

In a very short time, sentences will be appropriate for practice. It is important to use the same modeling process you used with the single words. Say the phonemes as you are writing them, and then say the word as a whole when you have finished writing it. After the entire sentence is up on the board, read it slowly and carefully, running a pointer or your hand under the words as you read them. Have the students repeat after you or with you. Obviously your sentences will be very limited and somewhat contrived, but this is only a temporary hindrance.

Remember to introduce all sounds and any sight words that might be needed before they show up in a sentence for your students to read. Their names are an exception to the rule because they are already working hard on recognizing and writing those. They will only be responsible for their own names. Using the students' names does wonders for keeping their interest high. For example, "(Student's name) sees the sheep."

The structure and content of the sentences develop as sounds and letters are taught. "_____ keeps the sheep. _____ feeds three sheep." As a point of interest and to keep yourself out of trouble, be sure you allow enough time for each student to have his or her sentence. Everyone sounds out all the words of every sentence as you write it. Then everyone reads the sentence together. Read through all the sentences together again. Finally, each student gets to read his or her sentence independently, with as much teacher assistance as may be needed. This is important even if you do not use their names. Lots of support, lots of encouragement, and lots of praise help them believe in themselves. Then they get to erase *their* sentences. It's a big deal, although I've never been sure why.

It really does not take very long before the students start *reading* while you are writing, and very soon after that they will begin anticipating what you are writing. This predicting will serve them well as they develop their reading process. It can be great fun to act surprised: "How did you know what that word was going to be?" They are in fact developing their knowledge of the syntax used in the English language, and they really begin to think of themselves as readers and writers with incredible abilities.

## Active Phonemic Manipulating

Another very positive activity is the use of letter cards. (You can even color code them to match the chart.) Have one phoneme per card and a pocket chart or a little stand for putting the cards on to form words: (p ee k), (s ee k), (k ee p). This exercise further illustrates for the students the interplay between the letters and how those wonderful consonants can be put anywhere and still make the same sound. If you are particularly ambitious or have some wonderful helpers, you can make a set of six cards or enough for however many students you decide to work with at a time. Then, you can make a word, say it, and have the students find the letters and make the same word. Then, of course, everyone repeats the word. This further develops visual discrimination.

These cards can also be used as you dictate a word, and then they can "spell" it with their cards. When they are through, you spell the word with yours, and the checking process occurs and corrections can be made if needed. Blocks or tiles with letters are also great manipulatives and are easy to work with. Do not forget the magnetic letters on cookie trays, but remember this is not playtime. Provide only the letters and sounds you have taught because you want to give yet another opportunity to practice and reinforce what the students are learning.

## Segmentation

The above exercise can be very helpful in teaching students to segment words. The reason you need to teach the skill of segmentation is because the ability to hear all the sounds in a word is important for both the reading and the writing process.

Another activity that helps develop this skill is to ask, "How many sounds do you hear in *sleep*?" Then put up your fingers as you count the sounds while sounding it out: *s ... l ... ee ... p*. Four fingers are up for the four sounds that you heard. Just a reminder, *sheep* would be only three sounds because sh- is a phoneme. (Together, *s* and *h* make a single sound.) Some teachers like to clap for each sound, and although it works well, it is not as useful as just counting with your fingers, because in a classroom setting, counting on one's fingers is much more acceptable than clapping. Teach them what is practical. Of course, it is possible that you will have a student who may need the added stimulus of the clap; in that case, go ahead and teach clapping.

## *Dictation*

Dictation should become your primary teaching strategy because you can incorporate so many valuable teaching principles within its scope. Dictation is crucial because you can include all the best practices: front-loading, direct systematic instruction, guided practice, and instant feedback within the context of small groups so you can monitor the children's mastery of the concepts that you are teaching. Just remember, don't teach everything at once—just one skill at a time. Again, it is important to set the students up for success. Stay attuned to how your students are handling the information that you are teaching.

The sentences that you dictate will directly reflect what the students have already been taught and what you are currently teaching. Dictation allows you to include practice of the new, review of the old, and even a way to front-load concepts before they are officially introduced. As you will notice in the Materials Manual, the difficulty of the sentences increases and yet continually allows a review of the mastered concepts. Dictation is a very effective and efficient way to teach reading and writing skills because of the several modalities used at one time and because of the instant feedback that is so vital to learning concepts correctly.

Whatever you have the students practicing, you must be there with instant feedback, gently correcting so they practice correctly. Don't reprimand for mistakes; just help. Another idea to help you help your students is that when you dictate a sentence, read or say the entire sentence and then repeat it one word at a time, sounding out the word as the students are writing it. Try to sound out the words at the speed of the slowest writer. There is something about all of the senses converging at the same time that helps lock the information into place. Hearing you say it while sounding it out for themselves as they are writing it and seeing it all at the same time is very beneficial for most students.

Remember that most children want to please their teachers, and as long as they feel successful, they will continue to try. Be there to assist your students at every opportunity. Young children love to read and write their names, so dictate sentences that give them an opportunity to do so. Select the words you use in the sentences very carefully so you include only what you have taught. (See the Materials Manual, Sections 8, 9, and 10, for additional sentences.)

## *Front-Loading*

To front-load, you actually demonstrate the use of the concepts before providing the direct instruction that explains them. This process provides the students with some idea of how something works before they receive any actual instruction. Giving them some experience with a concept before it is actually taught creates some prior knowledge of it. It is very similar to pre-teaching except that you expose them to the idea without any explanation first. In addition, you give all of your students the benefit of recognizing what you want them to learn. This helps make the concept seem more familiar, and ultimately it makes more sense to the students. You can include additional concepts as you feel your students are ready for them by using the same methodology. Please see the Materials Manual, Section 4, which demonstrates at what points teaching the various grammar concepts is most appropriate and effective.

## *Sight Words*

When you begin writing and dictating sentences, a few sight words will become necessary. Explain to the students that not all words play fair. (They probably know someone who doesn't always follow the rules when playing games.) Explain this carefully, and tell the students they must just learn the word by the way it looks. *The* is the first sight word you will teach. When you introduce *the*, you can show them how the first phoneme actually makes the sound it is supposed to; it is just the vowel that is confused. (Point out the th- phoneme in the voiced column.)

Write *the* somewhere your students can easily see it and close to the phonics charts that you use. You want it to be accessible at a glance. Use *the* frequently in the sentences that you dictate. Let the students become comfortable with it.

Add a new sight word when the students are ready. Do not let sight words become the focus, though. Just add one at a time as they are needed and as the previous sight words are mastered.

When students are first writing and reading sight words, have the ones you have introduced written and posted somewhere close to the charts so they are easily visible to your students. It sometimes saves time if you just start with a poster-size piece of paper and call it something like the "Most Wanted Words," the "Jail," or the "Penalty Box"—anything that might help the students remember that the words on the poster are there because they do not play by the rules and must *just be remembered.* Then you can just add a word to the poster as you introduce it to your students. Do not start out by listing all the sight words you expect them to learn. Remember, you are setting them up to succeed. You do not want to overwhelm them and give them a reason to quit. You also do not want sight words to undermine the confidence you are building in your students. So be sure those you teach are readily available to your students and are words they can use and practice in their sentences with you. You will be surprised when, in no time at all, they announce that they don't have to look at the word anymore because they know how to write it. Compliment them on their knowledge *but* leave the words up and available because some of your students will still be learning. Concepts become familiar when they are used, and thus the concepts are mastered through practice.

## *Grammar*

As you use or exercise the sounds by dictating sentences, you can also incorporate many of the important grammatical rules as well. Introducing grammatical concepts will look a bit different from the way you introduced the phonemes and the sight words. You model both capitalization and punctuation every time you write a sentence for them, and now you will begin to call their attention to it.

### Capitals

Demonstrate what a capital letter looks like and that it is always used at the beginning of a sentence. For the next few days, remind students about it and then begin asking them, "What do we put at the beginning of a sentence?" It doesn't take long before everyone is using capital letters at the beginnings of sentences. Another trick is to comment on how Paul remembered to use a capital letter at the beginning of his sentence. Instantly, everyone will have a capital letter at the beginnings of theirs. It is a slam dunk after one or two remember. After a few weeks, you can work on capital letters for names. This can be taught by pointing out that they use capital letters at the beginnings of their names. Explain that everyone's name begins with a capital letter, just like theirs.

## Period

Punctuation can also be encouraged in the same way. Begin work on just the period. At first it works well to write a sentence on the board with the period and explain to your students why it goes there. Do this for several days when you are writing sentences, pointing out why you are putting the period at the end. Once they are somewhat familiar with the idea, then instruct them with the full explanation of when and why it is used (only in regard to sentences, not abbreviations). Remember, you will have to give the explanation more than once and gently remind them about where the period goes.

## Plurals

As with many other concepts, you can model this idea and practice it before you actually teach it. The reason for making a point of it here is to help make understanding the difference between the -s and -es easier. If you will notice, -s, -z, -x, -sh, and -ch are all close together on the consonant chart. Point this out to your students, and if necessary take a piece of highlighter tape and create a box around those four phonemes. Explain that when you want to make words mean more than one and when the word ends in one of these letters, you add -es instead of just -s. It is also helpful, when you are dictating, to emphasize the difference with a little extra stress on the last syllable—dish*es*, etc. You will not need to do this forever, just until they get the idea of which words need -es at the end in order to be made plural.

The charts are really wonderful teaching aids, and although I do not like defacing materials, it is often helpful to make some notes and add some cues directly on the charts. When teaching plurals, you can use a marker to draw a box around the phonemes. Laminating gives the charts some additional use time too, but in the end, a new one every year is nice if you can fit it into your budget because fresh and clean are a nice way to start off each new year. The charts are relatively inexpensive and are a wonderful tool. If you can plan on getting a new chart every year, that's best because they do get used and affectionately abused.

## Apostrophe

When it is appropriate—that is, when all the previous concepts are mastered—you can teach possessive apostrophes. Students love these because you can show them how they can write less. Everybody loves a shortcut. Front-loading works well with this concept too. Write "Mat's hat" on the board, have the students copy it, and dictate the rest of the sentence. After two or three lessons of having them copy the possessive, teach the concept. You won't get much trouble from the students when you explain that they can write, "This hat belongs to Mat" or "This is Mat's hat."

As a point of reference, I would not teach contractions before the end of the first grade because each contraction is different. But once the possessive is mastered, then you can begin to teach the more obvious contractions. You can decide which one might be the most useful and start with it. Whichever one you decide on, write out the two words, such as *do not*, and then show your students how to eliminate one of the *o*'s by inserting the apostrophe so they end up with *don't*. Again, add one contraction at a time until they have a few of the more common ones under their belts. Then explain the rule and how it works and continue incorporating contractions into your dictation sentences and monitoring their progress.

## Suffixes: -es, -ing, -ed

To help students understand the suffixes -es, -ing, and -ed, they must understand the concept of present and past tense. Give them lots of examples, and demonstrate and model both the tense and the suffix. You will work on this concept over several weeks, introducing it initially and then reviewing and practicing it. Jump up and down and say, "I am jumping," and then write the sentence on the board. Say, "I jumped," and write that sentence on the board. You can do the same with other verbs. For now, just stick to the verbs that use -es, -ing and -ed.

As a word of caution, please do not even consider any irregular conjugated verbs such as *write/wrote* or *see/saw* at this point. They will come later. The students need to master the regulars before they get confused with the irregulars.

## Double the Consonant

A possible area of confusion is when to double the consonant at the end of a word before adding a suffix. The rule is that when a short vowel is followed by a *single consonant*, the consonant has to be doubled before a suffix is added. Some examples are *hop,* which becomes *hopped,* and *hit,* which becomes *hitting.*

What confuses the students is when the short vowel is followed by two consonants such as in *milk*, which becomes *milking*, and *land,* which becomes *landing.* This is further compounded by the consonant digraphs because, as you will recall, in digraphs, the two letters work together as one phoneme so your students cannot *hear* the two consonants at the end. This makes them unsure of what to do. Direct instruction is absolutely necessary to help clarify this concept. Model it on the board, show the students how it works, and allow them to practice it with you so you can give them feedback. They need to know if they are getting it. Always be ready to review and explain if necessary. The two questions below might help you clarify the rule for your students. There is also a mnemonic clue to help demonstrate the difference between what they hear and what they see. It is a bit confusing when the voiceless consonants are involved. See Chapter 6, A Potpourri of Ideas, for more information on mnemonics aids.

**Two Questions**

One method to help the students work through the doubling of consonants is to give them two questions to answer before they add a suffix.

1. Is the vowel short?
2. How many consonants are following the vowel?

This will be one of the few times you will tell them not to listen for the sounds but to actually count letters. They will need to see the word before they can make a decision. At first, of course, you will write the word because you and your students will be working through this process together. Teach your students to always write the word and then ask the questions before they add the suffix.

If the answer to the first question is no, add the suffix. If the answer is yes, then ask the second question. If there are already two consonants, just add the suffix. If there is only one consonant, then they know what they have to do—double the consonant so they can add the suffix. This is another concept that is easier to learn if you front-load your students by modeling it for several days in the sentences you write. Continue front-loading by telling them what to do as you dictate sentences to them. Then, once you have set the stage, actually instruct them on the rules of use. When you finally teach the concept, write many examples on the board, reviewing the idea over several days before you have your students practice it independently.

## Hearing vs. Seeing: Past Tense

Because the English language is fraught with pitfalls and often seems to delight in confusing those who would attempt to use it, it's anything goes when it comes to helping our students master some of the difficult areas. I say we do whatever it takes—have a no-holds-barred attitude.

ELL students, along with those who have trouble processing sounds, have a difficult time with our past tense -ed because it often sounds like -t. You will notice on the chart that -t and -d are a voiceless-voiced pair. That is, they are pronounced exactly the same way except for the use of the voice or lack of it. This is what happens when a word ends in a voiceless consonant. Our tongues, lips, etc., go into the position for the past tense form; however, in the interest of time (and lack of effort), we do not turn our voices back on, and the past tense -ed comes out sounding like -t.

To help students comprehend this, I draw an eye and say "looks like," and then I write the word correctly. Next, I draw an ear and say "sounds like," and I write the word the way we actually pronounce it. For example, under the eye I would write *hopped,* and then under the ear I would write *hopt.* Or under the eye I would write *jumped,* and under the ear I would write *jumpt.* It gives the students a clue as to what is really going on because we spend a lot of time telling them to sound out the words and then they feel we've thrown them a curveball. But an explanation and some practice clears up the confusion. So the rule is that if a word ends in a voiceless consonant followed by the suffix -ed, the suffix will be pronounced as -t.

## Drop the Final *e*

Once the basic spelling pattern of CVCe is established and understood, it will be necessary to teach your students to drop the magic *e* when they need to add a suffix to change the tense of the verb. They already understand tense because you taught it when you were working with the short vowel verbs.

Take time to teach them that the -ed denotes past tense and that, although you are in reality just adding a *d,* you have to know that the *e* is being dropped because if you didn't drop it, the word would be changed into a nonword. For example, *hope* would become *hopeed,* which is not a word. So the final *e* must be dropped so the word will remain a word once the -ed is added. As always, a little modeling and practice will make it a done deal.

To assist your students when you get to this particular concept, convey the following:

- Spelling Rule: Drop the *e* and add the suffix. Example: *hope* changes to *hoping* or *hoped*
- Reading Rule: When there is one consonant before the -ing or the -ed, the vowel says its name. Example: *hope* becomes *hoping* or *hoped* When there are two consonants, the vowel makes a short vowel sound. Example: *hop* becomes *hopping* or *hopped*

## Concepts Come and Concepts Go

Just remember to not teach everything at once and to practice whatever you teach. It is absolutely crucial in the beginning. However, as you continue to add to the amount of information you are teaching, it becomes increasingly difficult to review everything every day. So it is important to go back and review periodically even after concepts are mastered because no matter how well the students may know something, they can easily forget it if they stop using it. They are learning a lot of new information, and sometimes some of what is learned later "buries" what was learned early on. Even though you are teaching to mastery, the information has only been learned this first time, and with all the new concepts you are continuing to teach, the older concepts fade into the background, so to speak. This means that what your students are working on right now is what they know right now. Don't be discouraged if they forget a particular concept they had previously mastered. Usually, a reminder and an opportunity to practice it again will make the concept an operational skill again. It really isn't forgotten; there are just a lot of new concepts on top of it, pushing it farther back in the memory bank. That is the reason you must constantly review and practice what you teach.

## *Beginning Reading*

Once your students have mastered all the consonants and are hard at work on the short vowels, you will need to consider reading material for them. It is absolutely critical that what you have them read matches what you have taught.

Because this is so important, writing short stories yourself and having the students make their own from your dictation is the easiest way at first. It is only for a short time, but keeping the materials consistent to what you have taught is very important at the early stage of the reading process.

### Teacher-Student Books

A good technique is to make work sheets in advance and have the students illustrate them, demonstrating their comprehension. Divide a blank piece of paper into quarters. You can cut the paper into quarters or just fold it. At the bottom of the quartered paper, draw a line for their names and then write the sentence you want them to read, such as " _____ sees the sheep." On the next page, write "_____ feeds three sheep." (Their names go in the blanks just as when you dictate sentences.) Obviously, in the first one, they would draw themselves looking at a sheep, and in the second one they would draw themselves feeding three sheep. At first, when the vocabulary is rather limited by the "known" sounds, you may do just a page here and there. As the students learn more and more sounds, you may want to staple the pictures together into a little booklet. After it is completely illustrated and the students can read it well, it can go home to be shared and practiced. Your students will be working toward reading personalized mini stories.

As your students become more proficient in their ability to write what you dictate, prepare the paper prior to the lesson and then dictate a sentence for each of the squares. Have the students write one sentence on the bottom of each quarter page. If you are able, make the dictated sentences sound at least vaguely like a story—for example, "_____ sees three sheep. _____ keeps the sheep. _____feels the three sheep. _____ feeds the sheep." Then the students can draw pictures to illustrate the story and practice reading their books. The cartoon strip mentioned earlier can also be used here to reinforce the idea of correct sequence. See Section 8 of the Materials Manual for more examples.

## Controlled Readers

Once the students have really mastered the consonants and -ee- and have begun to study their first short vowel sound, you will need to be alert to their eagerness to read. When that first short vowel sound becomes familiar, bring out *Max the Cat* or whatever -a book you might have available. Regardless of the book's value as far as literature is concerned, the students become ecstatic as they actually read a real book. (Hopefully, it will have some semblance of a story line.) Please remember, this is a process, and the whole procedure is going to take several months to get to this point. Move slowly and steadily, giving the students time to synthesize each additional level of difficulty and information. Remember the old adage "How do you eat an elephant? One bite at a time"? It is quite appropriate when discussing how to teach reading and writing. Your students need to chew and digest what you are teaching them, and that takes time.

Modern Curriculum Press has several series in which each book emphasizes one vowel sound. This allows you to give the students the opportunity to start putting to use what you have been teaching because the sounds in it are very limited and predictable. It is important to always introduce the book by reading and discussing it with them before they read it for themselves. Read it to them several times, and then invite them to read it with you before they try it on their own. In actuality, you want them to almost memorize it before they read it independently because you want them to feel successful and to practice correctly.

Be very aware that the prepackaged books do not always follow the same sequence that you are teaching. Make sure that you have introduced all the sounds and sight words used in the controlled readers you give to your students to read. Yes, this does limit creativity, but it is only for a short time, and the benefits down the reading road are enormous because your students become confident in the letter-sound cueing system. They will use it without hesitation later. There is a certain amount of risk taking in reading, and you want your students comfortable enough with the system that they will continue to give it a good try as it gets harder. In the beginning, you need to minimize the risk factor because if they feel they are failing, they will give up before they give themselves a chance to succeed.

As I mentioned, there isn't a lot of literature in these first books, but if you infuse a great deal of enthusiasm as you read, the students will love them. You will read each book a few times, and then the group will read it together several times, with you tracking the words for them. The last step is for them to read independently, with you ever ready to assist. They love to read these very easy controlled readers because they truly recognize the words, and the pictures are great for giving plenty of context clues. The students' sense of accomplishment by really reading is a wonder to behold. You have set them up for success, and they love it.

**Now it is time for practice, practice, practice.**

## Buddy Reading

Buddy reading at this point is very beneficial. This can be done in any number of ways:

- Students within a class are paired to read together, called partner reading.
- Older students from another grade level and class can be paired with the beginners. This can be beneficial on every level, providing opportunities to make cross-age friendships and a reason for older students to practice their reading.
- Volunteers, parents, or elderly members of the community who have some extra time and love to share it with children make great partners.
- Any really patient person can be a reading buddy.

Your goal at this point is to allow your students as much reading time as possible. Should you use others to buddy read with your students, be sure to spend a few minutes explaining the purpose. You want everyone on the same page. Whoever is being the buddy must recognize the importance of positive assistance and encouragement. The "reading with" idea is just that—reading *with* them. If the student is struggling with sounding out the words, then the buddy should read *with* the student, not pressure him or her to sound out the word. To put it bluntly, you do not want some well-intentioned person undoing what you have been working hard to develop. Whoever helps read with your students must be aware that part of their job is making sure the students feel successful.

Being a reading buddy can be a great role for less efficient older readers. However, be sure that your older readers are far enough ahead of the younger ones so that they will not get caught in an embarrassing situation. The idea behind this is that everyone comes out a winner. When older students are paired with beginning readers, they should be the experts because they will be helping novice readers while at the same time practicing their fluency with texts they wouldn't read on their own. By helping the beginning readers with their stories, the older readers further develop their own fluency.

## Individual Oral Reading ... NOT!

Concerning reading in class, *please* try to avoid having individual students read out loud in groups or to the class. The reasons are probably fairly obvious. First of all, if you allow one student to read, then all should have a turn. But you do not want all of them to have a turn because you want your beginners to hear only really efficient reading. You or another very good reader—either an older student or another adult—needs to model the reading process. The other almost equally important reason is that you do not want the students to become too aware of how they are reading. Put plainly, you want to avoid Suzie becoming known as the best reader in the class and Johnny being identified as one who can't read. Competition has its place, but not here.

Remember, the focus is that *everyone* can read, and if some of the less mature students hear the advanced Suzie read aloud, they may become discouraged before they give themselves a chance. As much as possible, keep the playing field even, encouraging all the students and focusing on developing the reading process for everyone. Besides, if only one student is reading at a time, that means only one student is practicing, and that's a lot of wasted time. Stick with the choral reading, where everyone practices.

If you want to hear a specific child read, then be that child's buddy when you do buddy reading. It is a very good practice to do that on a regular basis anyway. Over the course of a week, you can hear all of your students read once or twice without doing the round-robin thing.

## Stages of Reading

There are three different stages at this juncture of the reading process, and students sometimes vacillate between them.

The first stage is *listening*: it involves their need to track and listen (you can do this in your small groups). The book you are reading should be held so the students can easily see it, and your finger should move along under the words while the text is being read. Or each child can have a copy of the book you are reading, and they can track independently while you read. Either way works; just be sure that they are on the right page if they have their own books. (You are always monitoring.)

The second stage is *with*: while the students are sounding out the words, their partners need to be reading out loud with them so the students can hear what they are reading. Hearing the correct sounds as they are sounding out the words is very helpful. The auditory reinforcement of what they are seeing and saying is quite beneficial in this beginning stage. It also helps to keep them moving without belaboring the process. Any adult who has some extra time can be a great resource by reading with a beginning reader. A little push and lots of encouragement goes a long way.

A variation of the strategy just mentioned and a very effective way to jump-start the reading process is choral reading or guided practice in small groups where everyone is reading together with the teacher. The only real difference from the activity described above is that sometimes the more efficient readers will push just a little, so you as the teacher must try to strike a balance by keeping it moving but not leaving anyone behind.

Finally, the third stage is *reader*. In this stage, each student reads to someone, and that person mostly serves as a listener and provider of moral support. As mentioned earlier, the students move back and forth through these stages; the difficulty of their reading material and their familiarity with the texts determine which stage they are in and the level of support they require.

Be prepared to allow for the movement, and be ready to support your students with the techniques and strategies that will be the most useful to them and their current needs.

## Pacing

It is very important to note that you do not want to rush the beginning readers. Remember, reading is the *key* to success in school. If beginners are shoved out of the picture books with all of the helpful picture clues too quickly, frustration and discouragement follow. This unfortunately decreases the amount of pleasure students get during reading time, which results in a less efficient reader later. The reluctant readers will read less just because it's too much work and they feel little or no success. Give your students as much time as they need to hone their skills. As long as they are reading, let them. Occasionally, a little nudge will be necessary, but do it with great care and monitor closely for frustration and discouragement. The time spent in the various stages of reading differs for individuals, and usually the students will know when they're ready to move on. As their interests change and mature, so will their reading materials.

## Classroom Organization

### Scheduling Time

As you cannot do all of the activities in a single lesson, one suggestion might be to do the chart work every day. It is a quick way to bring the lesson into focus, it serves as a reminder for the letters and sounds already known, and it sets the stage for the new sounds students are learning. Then use a set of letter cards (no pictures) corresponding to the sounds you are working on in the same sequence as the charts. At least one set of single picture cards should be used for the same reason and in the same order. Do this until you've worked through the short vowels; after that, the letter cards and pictures do not seem to be as important. Then choose at least two other activities, such as a picture game, some dictation, some board work, or some work sheets for exercise. Always end by reading at least two or three stories for fun.

With this approach, you will initially be working with a lot of pictures. At first, the students will deal with comparatively few letters, and twenty minutes will probably be a sufficient amount of time. Within a few weeks, as you add more sounds and the students develop their knowledge of the graphic-phonemic system, you will need to schedule more and more time. Around the midpoint of the year, especially when you begin working with the short vowels, forty-five to sixty minutes may not seem long enough. I know your initial reaction may be, "I can't spend that much time on phonics." Very seriously, I ask, can you afford not to spend that much time? I know there is a multitude of wonderful units and themes to teach, but I also am fully convinced there isn't anything else even half as important. The earlier and the stronger this foundation is laid, the better for everyone, especially those beginning students who so desperately need access to the reading process.

## Teacher Continues to Read

It is important that you continue to read real literature and stories to your students. You want to be sure that they recognize the reason they are working so hard to learn what you are teaching, and you want to continue to develop all the other skills that are required to be good readers. So when the smoke clears at the end of each lesson, be ready to reinforce and reward your students with a couple of good books.

At this early stage, picture books and repetitive books are really wonderful to read to your students. Introduce several books, one at a time, and put them in a tub or a basket. Then, after you have several books in the tub, let two or three students choose what you read. Be sure that each student in each group has equal time so that everyone gets a turn over the course of the week. Read with all the enthusiasm and excitement you can muster. Not only are you in charge of teaching the skills your students need, but you also *must* motivate them and give them a reason to want to learn to read. Reading is just so much fun! As you read some of the predictable books, they're going to want to guess (never mind that you have read it three times already). Let them have the fun of "guessing." Actually, they are demonstrating recall, which leads to comprehension, which is an important skill and should be encouraged.

## Consider Centers

One possibility is to break the activities into centers or stations, but then it would be *very important* to have an adult or a very responsible older tutor at each center. Remember, instant appropriate feedback is crucial to your students' learning this reading process correctly.

Your classroom might look something like this: you, the teacher, will be instructing the students with the new sounds, letters, and pictures; dictating the sentences; and reading a story or two. A second group of students might be working at a table or at their desks, drawing pictures of words or sentences they previously wrote during dictation or that were prewritten by the teacher, including only the sounds the students have been taught. A third group of students might be working with premade flash cards, practicing sounds they have been taught and even including sight words that have been introduced. A fourth group may be enjoying some "reading" time in the library corner. If personnel and space allow, a group could be reading appropriate words or sentences (prepared by you) written on a board or chart. Virtually any activity that allows the students an opportunity to see, hear, read, or write the phonemes yet again is to their advantage. However, it is really important that the students be monitored. At this point in time, you want them practicing everything correctly so they do not form bad habits that they will have to unlearn and then relearn correctly later.

There is no reason to add confusion to the reading process; it is complicated enough. There just isn't any substitute for supervision, assistance, and encouragement while they are learning to break the code. Think offensively and intervene before the fail cycle has a chance to get started.

## Nonreading Centers

If there are constraints that do not allow for every center or station to be manned by someone you feel will adequately supervise and assist the reading process, then you may want to consider non-reading centers. These centers might be the perfect place for students to work on some of the other skills they need to develop, such as coloring, cutting, pasting, or even improving their penmanship (practicing forming letters or writing their names or other prewritten words). There are a host of visual discrimination activities that would be beneficial to your students. They can practice many concepts and skills that won't jeopardize their reading and writing learning later. They can work with math manipulatives, patterning, colors, shapes—anything that is not part of the foundation for developing the reading and writing skills. You do not want them writing in journals and guessing at how words might be spelled or trying to read unassisted. This does not mean they shouldn't be looking at books, but you do not want your students guessing about any part of the reading and writing process at this crucial time.

Units or themes that would be interesting to your students could serve as the basis for one or two of your centers. If they are organized and presented carefully, they could give your students more opportunities for a greater variety of concepts and provide the basis for additional vocabulary development as well. An example might be reading and discussing community helpers for a few days and then focusing on one a day. The students could draw pictures of what the helper does. There could also be a listening station that could include a story about the helper. This idea could work well for the study of many other theme-oriented concepts.

When developing centers, please think ahead and determine whether the skill for each center will be required as part of the reading and writing process, and therefore requiring supervision for accuracy and correctness, or if it is a concept that is just something that is nice to know or practice. Thinking through what the purpose of the center is will help you determine the level of support the students need at each center and whether or not it will be appropriate at this time considering their skill level.

# Chapter 5:   Clarifying Strategies and Older Students

## *Sight Words*

Sight words are the culprits that probably helped give phonics a bad rap in the first place. It's rather amazing that approximately 80 percent of the English language is very phonetic, but several hundred of our most-used words are in the 20 percent that are not. Words like *the, were*, and *are* do not play by the phonetic rules. Most likely the easiest and most effective strategy is to just explain these as "poor sports." As was discussed in Chapter 4, a special chart can be used (made to look like a jail, a penalty box, or a time out area that's used by players when they foul out of a game). Do not put a chart with all the sight words on it from the beginning. As new sight words are introduced, add them to the chart. Keep this chart in plain view so the students can readily refer to it, just like the consonant and vowel charts. Flash cards have also served many a useful purpose; just make a card for each word as you introduce it to your students. When you have a few cards, rubber band them together and use them occasionally for extra reinforcement and practice.

My own personal belief is to not hold kindergarteners and first graders responsible for the spelling of the non-phonetic words. Keep these words accessible or spell them if you're dictating and need to use a word. First of all, most of your students will quickly pick up on the words just through use, which is great, but your first and primary focus is that your students master the graphic-phonemic sounds that play by the rules. In other words, first concentrate and focus on the rules, and then after those are mastered, the students can begin to deal with the exceptions. If an error is made either in reading or writing, blame it on the word: "Oh my, that's one of those words that doesn't play fair, remember?" There should be no pressure on the students for the first two years. Keep the affective filter low; if there's too much stress, learning cannot take place. You are already asking a lot. Keep in mind that some of your students may not have seen a book before they came to school. When you really analyze the letters, you find that several are very similar: consider *h, n,* and *r,* and then check out *p, q, d,* and *b* and *a, o,* and *c.* Also, remember how similar the sounds are. Allow your students the time and the opportunity to learn to discriminate one letter from another and give them a chance to master what's consistent. For one thing, they'll get so confident in the system that they'll attack any word, and if they get close enough (which is usually the case) they'll figure it out independently. Whether they are reading or writing, they will sound it out phonetically and continue on their way.

If, for some reason, students are having real difficulty with sight words at the end of the second or third grade, a program called *Instant Read*, which focuses strictly on sight words, can make quite a difference for students having problems with these rascally words. The program is also designed to promote fluency.

## Phonetic Sight Words

Not all of the hundred most-used words are phonetically incorrect, so teach the phonetic ones just like any other phonetic word. Have the students listen for the sounds they know. No one can learn everything at one time, so stay on track by teaching all the phonetically correct words first. You will find there are not many nonphonetic sight words that your students need for their beginning reading and writing practice. So wait until they need the nonphonetic words before you teach them, and remember to present them one at a time and with lots of practice.

## *Concepts Beyond Phonics*

Once students know the sound-symbol relationship, phonics is, by definition, completed. Phonics is the study of the sound-symbol relationship, which constitutes the basic or regular spelling patterns. However, there is still a lot to know about the English language and how it works, so if you are really interested in giving your students an extra boost, you can continue to develop their knowledge. The grammar and word studies can just pick up where the basic phonics ends. At approximately mid-second grade (as always, know your students), if they have mastered the regular spelling patterns, then you can use the same concepts that you have already been using: modeling, front-loading, direct instruction, and dictation, along with lots of practice to help students develop an understanding of many of the irregular spellings and grammatical rules that they will need to know. A progression showing when some of these concepts are most appropriate is included in the Materials Manual in Sections 4 and 5. It is by no means all inclusive, but if the concepts are learned thoroughly, your students will be well on their way to becoming confident readers and writers.

## Word Studies

Probably one of the best strategies for going beyond phonetic words is using word studies. This technique allows your students to learn and practice words that have a similar attribute, and through practice the irregular becomes known and understood.

Word studies could include irregular spelling patterns, prefixes, suffixes, root words, comparisons, and vocabulary work, which can be very beneficial and helpful to students. Some thought and time must be given to these studies if they are to be meaningful. Knowing how the parts of speech work gives students additional knowledge about the English language. Knowing about and being able to use words well and confidently is without a doubt a great asset to students as they move through the grades and encounter more complex words and language. Again, Sections 4 and 5 of the Materials Manual share possible concepts and ideas that promote knowledge and understanding of the English language and how it works. Just for the record, the progression is not set in stone; the guideline serves as an approximation. From many years of experience with students, this is about where the concepts fit into the reading and writing process.

## Front-Loading Through Dictation

The term *front-loading* was discussed in Chapter 4 as a strategy for teaching brand-new concepts in a learner-friendly way. Your students want to learn and to "get it right," so model the concept, giving them the opportunity to see it used. Through direct instruction, teach them the concept and then allow them time to practice it. Encourage them with instant, positive feedback. Include additional strategies such as a picture, a story, or a gesture. Often it is easier to understand something if we have had an opportunity to see it and even use it before we are given all the directions and information about it. This teaching strategy allows something to become familiar so that when the instruction follows, it makes sense and actually validates the students because they have already been doing it and now they know why.

Many concepts can actually be introduced and practiced during the dictation of sentences. It is a good way for the students to use these words and concepts correctly and get accustomed to how they should be used in a sentence. Your presentation of the concepts and your sentences can serve as a gateway for discussion that can generate even more language. Just keep your eye on the goal, with the big picture in mind. No matter what else you do, you want your students to know all the cueing systems and develop an understanding of how the English language looks and sounds, keeping in mind that their success and their feeling of achievement is what will ultimately make them the lifelong learners and readers we want them to be.

The purpose of this book is to get the reading process on track and moving, and since there are many very good programs that have already been developed, I will not try to reinvent the wheel. Modern Curriculum Press has some excellent materials, as will any good store or catalog that specializes in curriculum. However, do not let word studies and rules drive your reading program. They can and will suck the life out of reading, and an understanding of the reading process is and always needs to remain the ultimate goal.

Phonics should be mastered by the middle of second grade. Unfortunately, for any number of reasons, a few students will not have had the necessary exposure to phonics. They will not have been taught the correspondence between the letters and the sounds, nor will they understand the basic spelling patterns of the English language. Their knowledge of how the letters and sounds work will be impaired, through no fault of theirs, and it is necessary to help them learn how the language works and to help them redefine themselves as learners. The program as it is outlined in the previous chapters can serve as a remedial program. However, in the case of older students, you must be very careful to protect their dignity as much as possible by making the information look and sound grown-up. Remember that, despite any attitude they might give you, they know that they don't know how to read, so be positive; let them know that you do know how to teach and that if they work with you, they can learn to read.

## Assess

For the older students, the two big differences are speed and selective teaching. To begin, test the older students to determine what they know and what needs to be taught. Generally speaking, the three areas that are often the most problematic for older students are the voiceless digraphs, the short vowels, and the diphthongs. After analyzing a few diagnostic tests, you can determine the areas where students need assistance. There is no point in wasting teaching time with what they already know. (An example is the diagnostic test shown in Section 6 of the Materials Manual.)

## Remedial Instruction

For the older students needing remedial help, direct instruction with a minimum of fluff is the most efficient approach. Determine which consonants need to be taught; rarely do they need the single-letter consonants. The digraphs are, however, another story. So begin with one or two of those and the double -ee- vowel sound. Depending on your students, it may be permissible to give one short vowel sound, usually -a, right at the beginning along with the -ee- vowel sound to get the process moving more quickly. Just watch for confusion. Use the chart to share some of the tricks about voiceless and voiced sounds. Just that much often helps because the students had never been made aware of how similar many of our sounds are. Teach the sounds they need systematically and carefully, one sound at a time. You will not use the letter cards or the picture cards. Move through the progression for learning sounds, minimizing or skipping sounds they know and focusing on the sounds that they haven't learned.

For the older students, it is pretty much a "cut to the chase" situation. In the interest of time, teach the chart, dictate sentences, and monitor their work with positive, instant feedback. (They have been using these sounds incorrectly for too long already.) Have the students read back the sentences they write. And, as always, use the positive approach. For some, it is *critical* that you praise and encourage them. Work in small groups and monitor them while you dictate the sentences. Make sure they are "getting it." If there is a problem, help them in a reassuring way, accepting the blame if necessary, and repeat the word carefully until they write it correctly. I know this may be hard to believe—and in some cases almost impossible—but students really don't make mistakes just to upset you. Mistakes are made because the student does not know better, and guess what—that's your cue. It's your job; you are there to teach them. So assess your older students carefully and then systematically instruct them, moving at their speed and holding them accountable only for what you have taught them, *not* for what you think they should know.

If it becomes obvious that they do not know something, stop and teach it. Then plan to work it into your lessons as review so it becomes part of their knowledge base. It is very important that you set them up for success. These students have experienced enough failure. Now it's time to change their images of themselves and help them begin to see themselves as learners. So teach them the system and help them master it.

## Personal Chart

Sometimes having students make or giving them a copy of a premade chart as their personal chart is a big help, especially if they move between classes and the charts are unavailable in other classes. Both the consonant and the vowel charts have been used to great advantage in upper-grade classrooms for ELL students and others who are weak in spelling. They can be beneficial because all of the regular spelling patterns are displayed very clearly.

Teach from the charts in a matter-of-fact way, and give students as many clues to understanding how the English language works as you possibly can. Another idea for working with older students is to use overhead transparencies with or without the charts. The overheads are a great teaching tool because you can work on them and keep your eyes on the class. The overheads I created had the same basic information but no cute pictures. The charts covered the digraphs, diphthongs, etc. (See Section 5 of the Materials Manual for examples.) I found that the students liked knowing the big words, and as they began to understand how the letters and sounds worked together, they were much more willing to work at the reading and writing process. The overheads give it a very grown-up look and make it appear to be new information rather than a repeat of something they have already seen and didn't understand.

## Gestures Again

Many remedial reading students may have auditory processing problems, which is probably one of the reasons they didn't learn the system in the first place. Gestures can be very beneficial and even crucial to their success. My advice, after many years of experience, is to teach the letter, the sound, and the gesture, but *never* expect the older students to actually make the gestures. The gestures are going to be what you use to help cue the students. These gestures are usually necessary only for the vowels. I never needed gestures for the consonants with older students, but that doesn't mean there isn't a student out there somewhere who needs it. Once the students caught on to what we were doing, I would use the gesture when I dictated sentences, and then if a student requested the sound again, I would repeat the sound as I made the gesture yet again. As you develop a rapport with your students, you'll be able to know when they need the gesture and can supply the needed cue without verbal communication. Also, the vowel chart can be made to look more mature if you think the students need a more adult version. Just remember that all the regular spelling patterns in the English language are on the chart, and it is very important that students come to understand the concepts because that's how the English language uses the sounds. Once they understand how helpful it is, they really don't care. They are just glad to have some reference points and some understanding about this code that has caused them so much grief. See the Materials Manual, Section 2, for more information and examples.

## Basic Spelling Patterns

Once your struggling students get past the digraphs and short vowels, or whatever they needed the extra help with, you can often incorporate the rest of the class into spelling pattern practice. Be careful that you do not overwhelm the students you started out with because you want them to continue to experience success. Usually, several students in a class could benefit from a good review, especially if spelling patterns are taught and practiced. Unless you are specifically teaching a spelling pattern or some other aspect of the language such as homonyms, synonyms, comparisons, affixes, etc., you are probably wasting everyone's time anyway. So once the remedial students close the gap, you can then include the rest of the class as you teach the spelling patterns or other concepts if you think it would be beneficial.

## Comprehension

Students can know all the sound-symbol relationships and fully comprehend the language, but if they want to read well, they have to read. When students have to expend all their "brain energy" on decoding, their comprehension will, at best, be minimal. They work so hard to decipher the words that they lose much of the meaning. That is why the sound-symbol relationships *must* become automatic. The quicker and easier the decoding becomes, the more brain power is left over for comprehension.

The two big concepts that come into play here are automaticity and fluency. The bottom line is that the better the students know the sound combinations and the faster they can read, the better their comprehension will be. It goes without saying that without comprehension, there is not much point to the reading process. So it is imperative that we teach and have the students practice until the decoding process becomes second nature so that the more important aspect of reading, comprehension, can take place.

## Books

The next big goal is to get the students into books and reading. The reading process is like many other things in life: you have to practice to get good at it. "Practice gives confidence" is never truer than in reading.

For older students who are not already well into books and proficient in their reading process, it can be very difficult. Probably the saddest things a teacher can hear are "I don't like to read" from a student or, from a parent, "I can't get him to read." It's sad to say, but you can't force students to read. The real kicker at this point is finding interesting materials at a level they can actually read. Many magazines have fairly short articles, often with pictures, and the interest is high; however, at school it will be necessary to monitor which magazines are allowed, as some are more appropriate than others.

## Bottom Line

You can use all the motivational tools you have at your disposal. You can conference and negotiate strategies with parents and guardians for rewards for reading. However, in the end, the development of the reading process is the responsibility of each individual. As hard as it is, you need to tell your older students that now that they know how the sounds and the spelling patterns work, it is up to them. From this point on, it is a matter of their practicing if they want their reading to get better. Most students understand the importance of practicing sports—you can't run faster and farther unless you get out there and do it every day. Well, reading is the same way. They have to pick up a book and start practicing if they want to get good at it.

### Tutor

Sometimes enlisting a less proficient older reader to read with a beginning reader gives the older reader a purpose and adds to his or her self-esteem, and the end result is a more proficient older reader. If there isn't time in their school day or if younger students are unavailable, encourage your older students to read with a younger sibling or a younger relative or neighbor. Explain how important it is for the younger person to be read to and what a wonderful thing they would be doing for the youngster.

There just isn't any magic formula. It requires effort and time, and the truth is that the earlier the skills are developed, the better the chances are of developing readers. The reading process must be used to be efficient, and reading is the only way it can happen. It isn't impossible, but it is difficult; the older the students are when they learn how to read, the harder it is to become proficient.

## Second-Language Learners

This program works extremely well with second-language learners. It gives them a handle on all the important cueing systems and helps level the playing field.

For Spanish speakers who are older and proficient at reading and writing in Spanish, this method makes the transition quite easy. Spanish is a very phonetic language, and once the differences are discovered and the vocabulary develops, the connections are readily made so that English becomes very comprehensible and friendly.

# Chapter 6:   A Potpourri of Ideas

## Teaching Tips and Study Skills

As the reading process develops, the "reading to learn" phase begins to replace the "learning to read" phase because reading to comprehend and learn is what reading is all about. This chapter contains additional strategies and techniques that can assist students as they begin to read to learn. If you read any of the previous chapters of this book, you are already familiar with some of them. As with any strategy or technique, mnemonics can be adapted to a variety of needs. The examples given are somewhat reading- and writing-specific but can be adapted for learning many other concepts as well. Since study skills are so closely linked to reading, I have included a more comprehensive discussion on mnemonic strategies and how they can serve students throughout their education.

## Mnemonic Strategies

Mnemonics are aids that help recall information. Because the ability to retrieve information stored in the brain is often where the breakdown occurs that is the memory fails;

I have included several of the most successful and useful mnemonic strategies to help tap the information stored in the brain. Mnemonic devices help locate the information for use because they serve as a memory triggers or stimulus.

## Mnemonic Strategies: An Aid for the Memory

One reason mnemonics work is because they require engagement and some level of thought, which increases the possibility for active participation.

Four Reasons for Using Mnemonics:
- Provide context (organization)
- Enhance materials and make them more meaningful
- Provide specific retrieval clues
- Force the learner into an active learning position

Tips for Using Mnemonics:
- Keep concepts as concrete as possible.
- Help students visualize and picture the concepts.
- Offer variety; use different methods and modalities.
- Incorporate as many senses as possible.

It is necessary to model and practice the mnemonic strategies with your students. First, you teach the concept to them, and as they learn how it works, you continue to practice it with them. Eventually, you will have them come up with their own mnemonic clues.

## Most-Used Mnemonic Strategies

- Raps, rhymes, jingles, and poems with information - "i before e," "thirty days has September," etc.
- Signs, charts - the Golden Arches, the Taco Bell, phonics charts
- Alliteration: using the same first sound in a sentence - "Red to the right returning" reminds sailors to keep the red light on the right coming into harbor.
- Alphabet tricks: Using the alphabet to help remember - Putting lists in alphabetical order
- Acrostic: Each letter of a word means something - POWER = Prepare, Organize, Write, Edit, Rewrite
- Chaining: A form of acrostic, using the first letter of each word in a sentence. - "Please excuse my dear aunt Sally" reminds students of the order of math operations: parentheses, exponents, multiply, divide, add, subtract.
- Catchy phrases: Phrases that are easy to remember - "Righty tighty, lefty loosey" - For the word *stationary*, "*A* ain't going anywhere."
- Gestures: Some sort of hand movement or motion - Plate tectonics (slip, slide, collide) - The Bill of Rights: the number 1 looks like the letter *I*, and the First Amendment is about the individual having certain rights. Hold up two fingers like a Cub Scout for the Second Amendment, and then lower and point them so that your hand looks like a gun, reminding students that American citizens have the right to bear arms. Hold three fingers like the Boy Scout salute and notice that the tops of

the three fingers resemble a roof line, reminding students that no soldiers can be quartered in a private home without permission, and so on.
- Pictures: Photographs, drawings, sketches, etc. - "One picture is worth a thousand words."
- Color-coded materials and concepts

## Gestures

For very active students who have trouble standing or sitting still, use hand gestures to help them focus. These gestures may also serve as a mnemonic device for helping them remember the information. The use of gestures awakens the recall mechanism that triggers the memory and brings the information into use. Gestures do not seem to bother students who really don't need them and are dropped by the students who do as the information is mastered. It is difficult to understand exactly how the brain works because learning a set of hand gestures appears to be extra work; however, for those who need it, the gestures are a jump-start and a great help for retrieving information.

Gestures can be very useful for instructing students in the initial sound-symbol correspondence. The students who do best with this approach are the very active, very intelligent students and, yes, most often boys. For those who need some kinesthetic activities, this is it. If you have several students who may benefit from this technique, teach the gesture to the whole group—so no one feels singled out—and do the gestures yourself as you do the chart work. When you say "*p* says p-," use the simple gesture for p- found in the Materials Manual, Section 2. Try not to make an issue out of the gestures; use them but downplay them. Your students do not have to make the gestures; they are not mandatory, just extra. The gestures are an aid and should be used as such. You do not want them to become the focus of your lesson. If all of your students are attending well without gestures, then you probably don't want to use them at all.

It should be noted that for students who have auditory processing problems, gestures can be of great assistance. A visual cue can make a great difference for them. It may surprise you, but most of the students who have reading problems have auditory processing problems. For whatever reason, processing the sounds is a challenge. It isn't a hearing issue; it is a processing deficit. This means that we, as teachers, need to do what we can to make information more accessible by adding visual cues whenever possible. Having a chart up at all times and using gestures are two ways to help give these students more access to the information they need for developing their knowledge of the letter-sound correspondence that they need in order to learn to read and write. When gestures are used, it is important that you make the gesture in order to help the student make the connection between the sounds and the letters, not to make the students make the gesture. The Materials Manual, Section 2, outlines some possible gestures for helping teach the sounds.

**Pictures**

Another trick is pictures. Now, I am in no way an artist, but art is not the issue. What you want to do is help your students visualize spellings. Give them a gimmick, a handle, so they can remember yet another English peculiarity.

In Chapter 4, drawings of an eye and an ear were used to help the students differentiate between what is seen and what is heard when dealing with suffixes at the end of voiceless consonants that follow a short vowel. Pictures are a visual cue to help students understand the concept.

## *R*-Controlled Vowels

The *r*-controlled vowels are tough for some students because there is no way to hear which vowel is in the word, but for some of the more common ones, you can use pictures to help your students visualize the sounds. Make up your own for others that may be bothersome. For example, for the word *girl,* point out that *i* is the easiest vowel to make into a girl and proceed to do so. Add arms and legs and either use the dot for a nose and draw a head around it or use the dot for the head, whatever is easiest for you. Another example is the word *first.* Which vowel looks the most like the number 1? The letter *i,* of course. This is also an example of actually teaching the meaning of the word and the spelling with one picture. *Bird* can be demonstrated by drawing a tree with a little bird on a branch singing. (In my case, I always told them what I was drawing.) Then you explain that whenever people write music, they use notes. You proceed to draw notes coming from the bird and—oops! One of the notes fell down and dotted the *i.* *Turn* is also fairly easy to demonstrate. Begin by starting to write the *u,* and then ask students what they have to do if they leave home and then realize they forget something. As they tell you "turn around," you complete the *u* by "turning at the bottom."

First, teach your students that when they do not hear a vowel, that means the vowel is first and the *r* will come after it because the *r* is controlling the vowel—that is, it is not letting the vowel say its sound. So they are to write what they hear, leaving a space for a vowel in front of the *r*.

## Homonyms

Pictures can help with the understanding of homonyms as well. If possible, work with the letters within the words. It helps the students just that much more when they are reading and writing. Some examples are *see* and *sea*. Draw a pair of eyes and a caricature of a wave to represent the sea. Under the pair of eyes, write *see* and point out that the two eyes match the two *e*'s. Then write the -ea- for *sea* so the tail of the a is a little long and wavy like the waves of the sea. Usually, it is not that important to create pictures for both words because as long as students understand one, the other is a given.

For *peek* and *peak,* draw a pair of eyes and a mountain peak, and then write the words *peek* and *peAk* under the appropriate words. Give the explanation of *ee* and two eyes (again, you can use the picture to help with the definition of the word), which is helpful for recall. And in this particular case, if you use a little creative license you can write the *a* in capital form and help with the definition, which probably isn't necessary but is fun. Then there are *here* and *hear.* You can spend a minute discussing treasure maps, "*X* marks the spot," and how in *here* there is an *e* on either side of the *r,* which is where you would want to be if you were looking for treasure. For *hear,* draw an ear and show the students how *ear* is part of *hear,* which is what you do with your ears.

## *Storytelling*

A little storytelling can be helpful too, as you may have already noticed. This technique has already been demonstrated to some extent in previous chapters, like giving the students a reason for two vowels' helping each other make the long vowel sound. Little, short explanations that sound like stories are helpful. It would seem that putting the rule in story form gives it more context, and thus it is easier to understand and remember.

The single consonants are such that just the explanation of how they are made and the continued practice and use of them is sufficient. For digraphs, a little short story may help plant the sound and the letters a little deeper. For example, wh-, ch-, sh-, and th- are the four *h* brothers or sisters. They are quadruplets, and this is the way their mother tells them apart. *Wh* goes around *wh*istling all the time (if you or a friend are an artist, you can draw a picture of a child with his or her mouth puckered up for a whistle and the name *Wh*itney or *Wh*itaker underneath). The letters wh- written on the puff of air help emphasize the quietness of wh-. Be careful to pronounce the name correctly; wh- is voiceless, so be sure to distinguish it from the single letter w- sound.

Another sibling can be known as *Ch*arlie or *Ch*errie, and this child loves trains and is constantly making the train sound "ch ch ch." Have a picture with a child in a train engineer's hat and the chosen name written underneath. The third quad is the most polite of the four and always remembers to say "*th*ank you." This one's name can be either *Th*addeus or *Th*elma. And finally, the fourth quadruplet is named *Sh*elby, *Sh*ane, or *Sh*eri, and this one prefers everything to be very quiet because noise gives him or her a headache. So this child spends a lot of time *sh*ushing his or her siblings with the *"shhhhh"* sound, of course.

You can also make up stories for the various vowel sounds if your students need a little extra boost for remembering them. For more ideas, see Section 7 of the Materials Manual.

## Rhymes

Silly little rhymes sometimes are a big help. One such rhyme is, "We say menee; we spell *many*. We say enee; we spell *any*."

## Make Up a Saying

For words such as *model* and *label*, how can one remember if the ending is -le or -el? The little saying "tall short tall" can help. Both *d* and *b* are tall letters, as is *l*, while the *e* in the middle is short. Hence, tall letter, short letter, tall letter is the pattern students can follow.

Two more examples are the words *dessert* and *terrific*. If students remember the tiger that says, "It's grrrreat," they can remember that *great* is a synonym for *terrific*. So then they can remember that *r* is doubled, not the *f*. And then which would you want more of—desert or dessert? Notice which word has the double *s* in its spelling.

## Context Clues

If there is something within the word that helps, use it. It is difficult for some students to remember *there* and *their*. Point out that *here* and *there* are both places and that the word *here* is within the word *there*. And if you need to take it a step further, *I* refers to a person, and *I* is within *their*. The first example is usually enough to make the distinction that is required for using the correct word. In the case of *stationary* and *stationery,* it is easy when you say, "*A* ain't going anywhere," because you are in fact calling attention to the letter *a* within the word.

## Several Tricks for Magic -e

I prefer "magic -e" simply because there are other times when *e* is silent and doesn't make the preceding vowel say its name. When you write, make the *e* at the end of the word have a "tail" pointing back to the first vowel, which is supposed to say its name, and then show one hand over the ending *e*'s mouth, demonstrating that it isn't saying anything.

Another mnemonic trick when you are dictating a word with the magic -e is to use a loose fist, with the back of the hand facing you and the thumb up, and then point with the thumb like it's hopping over a letter to point to the vowel in the middle.

## Be Alert

Please remember that these are examples and ideas. You must get in the habit of watching your students, and then be ready with some sort of mnemonic aid to help them come to grips with the irregular and confusing aspects of the English language. Learn to look at words and think, "How can they be remembered?"

The rule is to do whatever it takes. The point is not good poetry or great art; in fact, sometimes, it is the goofy that helps the recall process. As you model and demonstrate the process, invite students to think up ways they might remember a particularly tricky word or concept.

Not every student will need these types of clues. What is especially important to note is that once the information goes into the long-term memory, the mnemonic device is dropped altogether. So please do not think you are going to have students doing these things every time they need to write a word. This process just helps jump-start the process for many students and allows them access to learning how to read and write with less stress.

Mnemonic devices are useful not only for helping to remember spellings and meanings but also for learning and recalling other information. In teaching students different ways of looking at words and learning them, you are also helping them to learn valuable study strategies that can be used for other subject matter later in their schooling. Again, invite them to participate and encourage them to figure out ways to remember the concepts they need to master the wonderful language of English.

## Graphic Organizers

Graphic organizers can be used as a tremendous help, both as a means of extracting pertinent information from a text and as a way to help organize thoughts prior to writing. Graphic organizers are also useful in helping develop critical thinking skills, which are crucial if students are to be able to move up through Bloom's Taxonomy and become independent thinkers and problem solvers.

### Critical Thinking Skills
- Patterning
- Sequencing
- Grouping and labeling
- Comparing and contrasting

- Synthesizing
- Analyzing cause and effect
- Recognizing relationships
- Making comparisons
- Summarizing main ideas

Samples of all the different types of graphic organizers are located in the Materials Manual.

## Graphic Organizer Examples

Below are some examples of how the various graphic organizers can be used. Again, the idea of mnemonics applies: picturing and organizing information is helpful when reading or writing for information and meaning.

Ideas for Using Various Structures of Graphic Organizers

**Spider Map**
Brainstorm
Organization of materials
States of matter
Phylum

**Continuum Scale**
Timeline
Sequence
Probability
Distances

**Compare and Contrast**
Classifications
Attributes
Polls
Same/different

**Fishbone**
Earthquake
Flood
Volcanic eruption
War
Any major event (what caused it, what happened next)

**Problem-Solving Outlines**
Social studies
Science

Math
Literature (plots in stories)
Major concepts with big changes or problems/how the solution was brought about
Government issues/crime, taxes

**Network Tree**
Main idea with details
Animal kingdom
Plant kingdom
Family tree
Federal government
Judicial system
Paragraphing

**Cycle**
Metamorphosis
Water cycle
Food chain
Plant growth
Life cycle
Seasons

## Fact vs. Fiction

First, students need to be instructed in the difference between fact and fiction, reality and pretend. Present a mini lesson on the difference, and then use some sentences or articles to help clarify the difference between fact and fiction. Another area that needs to be addressed is fact versus opinion and the differences between them. These concepts need to be introduced and practiced just like any other skill you want your students to learn. Magazine articles from *Highlights, Ranger Rick,* and *Owl* are great tools to help students look for examples of the different genres of writing. One simple strategy is to have the article printed on a transparency, and then you do not have stacks of papers to pass out to each student. Plus, transparencies store nicely for use year after year. If your classroom has computer technology, the articles could be downloaded for use with a PowerPoint presentation. The simple T organizer works very well to demonstrate fact and fiction; it has "Fact" on one side and "Fiction" on the other, and the objective is to list the points in the correct column. It may take some discussion at first because opinions can often be confused for facts. It might even be necessary to do a fact-versus-opinion lesson so students truly understand what a fact is and what it's not.

### Compare and Contrast

This important skill can be learned with either the Venn diagram for two items or a matrix for three or more items. Choose items to compare (stories, animals, sports, etc.) and then discuss how they are alike and how they are different. During the discussion, write the attributes in the appropriate area, indicating whether they are the same or different and why they belong in that particular area. As always, you will model the process on the board, and as students come to understand it, you will allow them time to do it on their own. But always end the lesson with writing the completed diagram or matrix on the board so all the students have access to a correct example.

## Cause and Effect

Another important aspect of reading is to distinguish between cause and effect, which often turns into a causal chain or the domino effect, in which one thing leads to another. The two organizers that are the most useful for cause and effect are the circles with the arrows pointing in (cause) and the arrows pointing out (effect) and the double herringbone with slanted lines on either side of the event or the happening. These concepts are important when reading and writing in all subject areas. The student's knowledge of cause and effect can determine his or her level of understanding of many of the ideas presented in science and history. I have included some graphic organizers that help students visualize these concepts, as well as structures for cycles and progressive steps for instructions that lead to goals. These graphic organizers are designed to help students see the concepts and ideas. Students can be taught to use these structures as visual aids and tools to further their academic success in all of their classes. Remember the teaching components: model, teach, practice, give feedback, and provide a correct final product for everyone at the end of the lesson.

In the beginning of the reading process it is all about *learning to read.* The rest of the educational reading experience is about ***reading to learn***. In other words once the decoding process is well established it is necessary to take your students to the next level of reading and teach them how to read for facts and information. The following activities and strategies can be helpful in maximizing their reading process to access the various academic texts.

## Active Reading for Information

**Warm-ups:**

Beginning
- Title
- Introduction

Middle
- Headings
- Subheadings

End
- Summary
- Questions

R double C = Read, Cover, Consider

Indentation notes: Put main ideas as the headings and then indent for the supporting details:
- Main Idea
  - Supporting ideas

Write notes in your own words.
Keep notes brief.
Use abbreviating symbols.
Be sure you understand your notes.

## Aspects of Reading that Should be Addressed as the Students Progress in Their Reading Skills

There is no definitive progression for what should be taught first or second; however, the degree of difficulty increases as the list progresses. But as with many skills and concepts, students should move back and forth between them, developing and increasing their skills at each visit. As their reading material becomes more difficult, reviewing certain skills will be necessary because each level requires greater expertise. You will recognize many of the skills from various chapters in this manual.

The following concepts are best taught through short, practical lessons. That is, they should be taught in context and with a purpose. Modeling and instructing the students in the concepts is the most efficient way to teach the graphics. And as always, varying amounts of practice will be required to master the concepts. Using real stories and expository text will demonstrate to the students the purpose of the skill. Those skills with an asterisk are particularly well adapted to a particular one of the graphic organizers.

- Vocabulary development and comprehension
- Sequence*
- Predicating
- Inference
- Confirming or adjusting ideas
- Alphabetical order
- Following directions*
- Reading and writing strategies
- Fact vs. fiction*
- Main ideas*
- Supporting details*

- Summaries
- Paraphrasing
- Fact vs. opinion*
- Generalizations
- Cause and effect*
- Compare and contrast*
- Reference materials
- Graphs and maps
- Propaganda*
- Idiomatic expressions
- Analogies
- Similes and metaphors
- Reading and writing perspectives
- Study skills
- Proofreading

### Reference Books

Dictionaries, thesauri, and maps and charts require different reading techniques, and the skills to use these references are very important if a student is to do well in all of the academic areas. But again, many have gone before me, and school supply stores have a myriad of books, workbooks, and activities to help develop and strengthen skills in these areas. So I feel that though I should remind you of their importance, you'll do well to put together your own units and programs depending on your students' ages and needs.

### Confession

I confess I did consider writing a chapter on teaching, but I have reiterated the most important concepts almost to the point of wearing them out. The bottom line for teaching students is to give them tools for learning and understanding, and those have been thoroughly covered. Using the teaching strategies explained in this book, you can teach just about anything to anybody.

## *The Most Effective Teaching Strategies*

- Modeling and demonstrating what you want students to learn
- Direct systematic sequential instruction
- Small groups (crucial for teaching skills)
- Guided practice for the skills that have been taught
- Monitoring with instant, positive feedback
- Mnemonics
- Teaching skills to mastery (lots or practice)
- Setting the students up to succeed (teach at their instructional level)

### Just One More Time

However, at the risk of repeating myself yet again, I feel compelled to remind you that just because a child is a particular age or in a specific grade, we cannot assume that the child knows certain things. There are many reasons students may not know what we think they should know at any given time. They may not have been developmentally ready when they were taught, they may have been exposed to poor curriculum, or there may have been a lack of instruction. They may have moved a lot, which means they were exposed to different programs and unfortunately were "plugged" into wherever their new class was in the reading process, and that means the students end up with gaps, areas in which they have never received instruction.

So *please* get to know your students. You may be the first and only positive thing in their lives. That does not mean you excuse them from learning; it means you work with them twice as hard and with lots of support and encouragement so they have a chance at getting into the business of learning. Assess them and then teach them at their functional level or—if you prefer the technical term—their zone of proximal development, which means that students have to have the background or the prior knowledge and the maturation before learning can take place. So be sure your students have the skills that are required for the new concepts you are teaching, and remember to use several modalities as you teach new concepts.

The good news is that the better students read, the more discriminating they are about what they read and the easier and more efficiently they read content area materials. Basically, the student who reads well learns well. Since no single thing is more important than the acquisition of an education, it is of extreme importance that every teacher do everything in his or her power to teach students how to read. The reading process is the ultimate key to the development of one's full potential in a technological society.

To add a little extra incentive for you, the teacher, I'll point out that the better you do your job and the better your students understand what you are teaching, the better they can work independently and the fewer behavior problems you will have. Over 90 percent of the behavior problems in classrooms occur because the students do not have the skills or the understanding to do their assignments. Some extra careful teaching at the beginning of new concepts can eliminate a lot of problems for everyone later.

Furthermore, self-esteem is directly related to the ability to read, so as the person responsible for teaching students to read, you have an awesome responsibility. How well they learn to read can truly affect the rest of their lives. (No pressure there.) Just remember that now you have resources, skills, and a knowledge base to teach them how to read and write with confidence.

For your convenience, you can obtain a CD of the *With Reading and Writing for All Materials Manual* as referenced in this book.

As you plan your lessons, you can have at your fingertips charts, rhymes, and hundreds of words and sentences that provide you with the information you need. Also, the manual includes examples of strategies and techniques for teaching the sounds and concepts that your students need for developing mastery. As a bonus, there is a page of all the basic graphic organizers for pulling information from text or for organizing thoughts before writing.

# Materials Manual Table of Contents

To order,
mail $12.00 (check or money order)
with your name and address to
Louise McGrew
10654 Ave 104
Pixley CA 93256